ROMANS
Vol. II
Living by Faith

Romans 6:1–16:27
by Theodore H. Epp
Director
Back to the Bible Broadcast

A
BACK TO THE BIBLE
PUBLICATION

D1122876

A Do-It-Yourself Course

14 units

published by
Back to the Bible Correspondence School
Lincoln, Nebraska 68501

78,500 printed to date—1977
(5-5903—75M—87)
ISBN 0-8474-2307-7

Printed in the United States of America

Instructions

Please familiarize yourself with these instructions before beginning your study of the lessons.

The first book in this two-part study of the Epistle to the Romans, entitled *Saved by Faith*, covered chapters 1—5 of this important letter from the pen of the Apostle Paul. A knowledge of the basic truths concerning salvation is needed for a proper understanding of God's love, justice and grace. It is recommended that you complete the first volume before proceeding with the studies in this second volume.

Not only are we saved by faith, we are also to live the Christian life by faith. This second series of studies in the Epistle to the Romans deals with this important subject. God wants every Christian to be a knowledgeable and mature believer, enjoying victory and bearing fruit to His glory. May these studies help you to put faith into action in your day-to-day living.

Study Suggestions

Preparation for Study

It is easier to concentrate if you have no distractions. Try to find a place where you can be by yourself, with no outside interference. If it is very difficult for you to concentrate, try reading the study material aloud.

Always pause to seek God's help before you begin to study. Ask Him to show you the significance of the truths you will be studying. As the author of the Scriptures, He wants to teach you more about Himself and His Word.

Materials for Study

A Bible. This is your principle textbook. This course has been planned to help you know your Bible better. The final authority is not the course of study but the Scriptures themselves, on which this course is based.

A dictionary. Use it whenever you encounter words you do not fully understand. Look up their meaning and usage.

A pencil, pen or marker. Underline important words and phrases. As you review the lessons later, the underlining will help you to quickly recall what you have studied. You will also need a pencil or pen to write in the answers to the exam questions. (Many persons prefer to use a pen for easier reading later.)

Method of Study

Begin your actual study by turning to the first unit and reading the lesson through quickly, noting especially the headings. Then carefully read it again, making a detailed study, looking up every Scripture reference. Study the unit until you have mastered it.

Each unit contains a memory assignment at the end of the lesson. Start working on this the day you start a new unit. Go over the verse or verses several times each day, repeating the reference before and after. This will help you remember where the verses are found.

As you study, think over the teaching presented, and apply the truths to your life. Pray that the Lord will show you how you can use these principles to help you in living for Him.

Turn to the examination, which is on the last two pages of the unit. Look over the questions to see how well you can answer them, but do not take the examination yet. Note what parts of the lesson you need to study further, and then look for the answers in the unit or in your Bible.

Taking the Examinations

After you have studied and carefully reviewed the first lesson, take the examination without using your textbook or any notes you have made. Where Scripture references are given in the questions, you may use your Bible in referring to the passages except where direct quotations are required to be written in the blanks. Memory work can be checked by reciting verses to someone or by writing them out on a separate piece of paper and then checking them with the Bible.

After you have completed the examination, check your answers with those given in the Answer Key, which begins on page 115. If answers do not agree, carefully review the part of the lesson involved and related Bible verses. Follow this same procedure when studying other units.

Planning Your Study

You can best tell how much time you should allow for each unit. But we recommend that you plan to complete one unit each week, if possible. Regular study is best, but don't worry if some units take longer than we suggest. You are wisely investing your time when you are studying God's Word.

4

Keep the examinations for this Do-It-Yourself Course in the book. Do not send them to us for grading. If you have questions concerning this course and have no one to help you, you may write to us at Back to the Bible Correspondence School, Box 82808, Lincoln, Nebraska 68501. We also stand ready to help you with any spiritual problem you may wish to share with us.

Contents

unit 1

What the Believer Must Know

The foundational truths for a victorious, peaceful, happy Christian life, are laid down in Romans 6. We may face troubles on every hand and yet have quietness and confidence in the heart. We will never be without testing and trials on this earth, but we can come through them victoriously.

Some will protest and say, "You do not know the circumstances under which I have to live." No circumstances can win out over the victory God provides. The Lord Jesus walked upon the waters when the storms were raging on the sea. In a spiritual sense, even though storms may be raging in our lives, we can walk on top of the boisterous waves with our hearts at peace, victorious over all circumstances. This is possible only as we comprehend through the help of the Holy Spirit these basic truths laid down in Romans 6.

Another name for the victorious life is the sanctified, or separated life. Some persons are frightened when we use the word "sanctified," but we must remember it is a Bible word. Others, again, are thrilled when they hear it; but they, perhaps, have some wrong ideas concerning it. The sanctified life is not a matter of feeling. We thank God for feelings. They are necessary, but they are not reliable proof in themselves with regard to the true state of the Christian life. The word "sanctify" means "to separate"; and it is the life of separation from sin unto Christ which is the subject of Romans chapters 6, 7 and 8. If we get the foundation laid properly for this truth we will lay the ground-work for spiritual growth.

We must not become discouraged if we do not see all of this truth at once. We will find, as did Paul, that there are obstacles in the way. We will also find that we will experience more victory from day to day as we understand more fully of the life of victory.

Before we take up these matters in detail, there are two facts which we should keep in mind constantly. The first of these is that in our fallen nature (the flesh nature) there is no good thing. We cannot change it for the better. There is no improving it. It will always be at enmity with God and the things of God. The other fact to keep in mind is that there is forgiveness in Christ for the sins we commit. There may be matters that we have hesitated to confess to Him because we have been guilty of sin in those areas before, but our Saviour stands ready at all times to forgive our sins if we will confess them (I John 1:9). When Jesus died for our sins, He died for all of them. He anticipated every one of them and bore the penalty in His own body on the tree.

With these facts clearly in mind, let us now investigate the life of victory in Christ. Romans 6 gives the doctrinal foundation, chapter 7 shows this life put to the test and chapter 8 reveals how victory is won through the power of the Holy Spirit in the life.

Doctrinal Foundation

The first verse of Romans 6 contains two questions: "What shall we say then? Shall we continue in sin, that grace may abound?" We see from this that someone has argued that if much more grace abounds where sin abounded (Rom. 5:20), then believers ought to sin more because the results will be more grace.

Paul answers this with a very emphatic denial and in turn asks a very important question which requires considerable explanation. His words are: "God forbid. How shall we that are dead to sin, live any longer therein?" (v. 2). In these words, he introduces us to the new relationship that the Christian has with the sin nature because of the finished work of Christ. The Apostle says we are dead to sin. Perhaps someone might argue: "That

10

is all right for Paul, but it is not for me. I am not dead to sin." But God says you are if you are a Christian. The next few verses in this chapter tell us who is included in the word "we."

Identified With Christ

The third verse introduces the word "know" which is one of the key words in this portion. Victory without knowledge is impossible. A believer lacking a clear grasp of the doctrinal background in Romans 6 will stay defeated in his daily experience. Other key words will be discussed as they occur in the text, but now let us consider what the apostle says we "know."

We read: "Know ye not, that so many of us as were baptized into Jesus Christ were baptized into his death?" Just what it means to be baptized into Christ is explained in I Corinthians: "For by one Spirit are we all baptized into one body . . . and have been all made to drink into one Spirit" (12:13). This is not water baptism, but Holy Spirit baptism. The Holy Spirit takes believers in Christ and places them into the Body of Christ, making them actual members of it. There is, in reality, a double action here, for we are not only placed into the Body, but as members of that Body, we have separate functions to perform.

The vine and the branch of John 15 illustrates this truth. It is hard to tell where the vine ends and the branch begins, but what we need to remember is that the branch is an outgrowth of the vine. The vine was first, not the branch. The vine has the life without which the branch could not grow. But the source of the branch is in the vine, which is the relationship that exists between us and Christ from the moment we were born again. We actually come out of Christ.

First of all, we were placed into Christ as the word "baptize" signifies. Water baptism pictures this. A person is placed into the water and then is brought back out of it.

In order to visualize this properly, do not think of the physical body of Christ in this connection, but rather think of Christ in the spiritual aspect in which He is present everywhere and is our life when we are placed in Him. Then, as one comes out of the waters of baptism, we grow out of Christ. Here is what the Scripture says, "For as many of you as have been baptized into Christ have put on Christ" (Gal. 3:27). The next verse in that chapter tells us that we are "one in Christ Jesus."

11

Another way to illustrate this truth might be in the realm of grafting. Suppose someone lacked an eye or was blind, and another person gave that one a live eye to be placed into his body. This would illustrate in part, at least, the truth here. One translator uses the word "incorporated" in connection with our being placed into Christ.

Such teaching as this gives no room for pride in any way. Our flesh nature is against such teaching because it likes to magnify itself. God says this is a new way of life, for in Colossians 1:27 we read: "God would make known what is the riches of the glory of this mystery among the Gentiles; which is Christ in you, the hope of glory."

The same truth is seen in II Corinthians 5:17: "Therefore if any man be in Christ, he is a new creature: old things are passed away; behold, all things are become new." If a person has been baptized by the Holy Spirit into Christ, he is a new creature, or new creation. For him old things are passed away and all things are become new. We sometimes interpret this to mean that all the old habits and temptations and sinful things have been taken away, and there will be no more temptations for us to face. But that is not what the apostle is dealing with. What he is saying is that the old methods, the old ways of trying to live by prescriptions and formulas and models, trying to make ourselves into what we ought to be, is now gone. Instead, we allow Christ to be in us and to be our life in us. It is a new way, God's holy way; it is the way of Christ in us, the hope of glory.

To be baptized into Christ, then, means to be identified with Christ in His crucifixion, burial and resurrection. This great truth we must know.

In saying that we have been crucified with Christ, the Scriptures do not teach that we bore our own sin. Christ was our substitute, He bore the penalty, but when He died we died with Him, and in so doing, we died to sin.

An observation that has helped me understand what it means to be dead to sin is that after Jesus died and was buried, rose, and ascended into heaven, He did not come in contact with sin any more. He, of course, never committed sin at any time, but when He passed into heaven He passed into another realm where sin cannot even come near Him, and He can no longer be judged for my sin. This truth as it applies to us is stated in verses 6 and 7: "Knowing this, that our old man is crucified with him, that the body of sin might be destroyed, that henceforth we should not serve sin. For he that is dead is freed from sin."

Perhaps we will see this truth more clearly if we read it from another translation: "For we know that our former self was crucified with Him (Jesus), to make our body that is liable to sin inactive, so that we might not a moment longer continue to be slaves to sin. For when a man is dead, he is freed from the claims of sin" (vv. 6,7, Williams).

It is clear from the Scriptures, then, that we who trust in Christ have been crucified with Him and are dead to sin. It is not that sin is dead, but we are dead to sin. So far as our experience is concerned, sin is very much alive, but we are to consider ourselves dead to our old nature so that it can no longer control us. Even though our sin nature has been nailed to the cross it still wants to dictate to us and get us to do the sinful things we used to practice before we knew Christ. But our fallen nature has no further right to us. We may listen to it, but if we do, we will fall into sin. We should consider ourselves dead to our fallen nature but alive to God. The sinful nature needs the body through which to practice its vice, and for this reason keeps after us to yield our bodies to it. No wonder the apostle wrote, "Let not sin therefore reign in your mortal body, that ye should obey it in the lusts thereof" (Rom. 6:12).

It is essential, then, that we know that we are crucified with Christ. To know this fact is basic for our entire study in this remarkable passage.

Note the results that should follow. The person who has died is free from the claims of the sin nature. Think of a man in a coffin. He cannot be tempted to sin any more because he is dead. Think of ourselves in that place for a moment. We are dead with Christ and have been buried with him so that sin has no further claim upon us. It is true that in our daily experience we can be tempted by the sin nature; but it is equally true that the sin nature has no claim or authority over us. Having been crucified with Christ, we are dead to the sin nature.

Memory Assignment:
Memorize Romans 6:3.

EXAMINATION

Complete the following.

1. Another name for the victorious life is the _____, or _____ life.
2. The word "sanctify" means "to _____."
3. Every Christian must expect to find _____ in the way of the life of victory.
4. In our _____ nature there is no good thing.
5. We must remember that there is _____ in Christ for the sins we commit.

Circle the correct letter:

6. In studying the life of victory, we find in Romans 6
   a. this life put to the test.
   b. the doctrinal foundation.
   c. explanation of how victory is won through the Holy Spirit.
7. In answer to the question, "Shall we continue in sin?" we are told
   a. that where sin abounds grace abounds more.
   b. that we are not capable of sinning.
   c. that we are dead to sin.
8. Victory is impossible without
   a. a knowledge of the facts in Romans 6.
   b. a knowledge of God's law.
   c. a strong will.
9. The "baptism into Jesus Christ" means
   a. water baptism.
   b. to be identified with Christ in His crucifixion, burial and resurrection.
   c. a special emotional experience.
10. The Scriptures teach that we have been crucified with Christ, and thus
    a. we bore our own sin.
    b. we died to sin.
    c. we will no longer come into contact with sin.

14

True or False:

11. _____ Sin is dead to the Christian.
12. _____ The sinful nature needs the body through which to practice its vice.
13. _____ To know that we are crucified with Christ is basic to the study of the life of victory.
14. _____ A Christian in daily experience can be tempted by the sin nature.
15. _____ The sin nature has only a limited claim on the life of a Christian.

☐   I have memorized Romans 6:3.

2+2 = 4

unit 2

What the Believer Must Reckon

Romans 6:8-10 brings before us a relationship that is very important. The words are, "Now if we be dead with Christ, we believe that we shall also live with him: Knowing that Christ being raised from the dead dieth no more; death hath no more dominion over him. For in that he died, he died unto sin once: but in that he liveth, he liveth unto God." The sin spoken of here is the sin nature, or the Adamic nature—which is also called "the old man."

In verse 11 we are told: "Likewise reckon ye also yourselves to be dead indeed unto sin, but alive unto God through Jesus Christ our Lord." Here is another way of stating this truth: "In the same manner you also are to account yourselves as dead men in relationship to sin, but as living men in relationship to God, as those whose lives are absorbed in Christ Jesus."

We have already seen that the word "know" is an important word in Romans 6. The second word of significance is in verse 11 and is the word "reckon." The word "reckon" simply means "to count something as a fact—to count it as true."

In arithmetic we know that two and two are four. We reckon that to be true. We accept it as a fact. This is true no matter where we go in the world, in China, Russia, Africa, or in our own country. It would be true even if we went to the moon. No matter where we go we reckon on that fact for ourselves.

Reckoning carries the idea that we count as true in our lives what we have come to know as facts. For example, we count it true that we (each of us personally who trust in Christ) have died to sin and are now alive to God. Just as I know that Christ died for my sin, so I reckon on this as being absolutely true for me. Before we continue deeper into the subject of reckoning, however, let us clearly grasp the following distinctions. They are vital at this stage in our study.

Two Important Prepositions

Our Saviour not only died for sin but He also died to sin. This second preposition is emphasized in verse 10. "For in that he died, he died unto sin once: but in that he liveth, he liveth unto God."

We were reconciled to God by the death of His Son. His death saved us from the guilt of sin and it is with respect to this aspect of the cross that we say Christ died for sin. According to Hebrews 1:3, He by Himself purged our sin; and again, in I Peter 2:24, we are told that He bore our sins in His own body on the tree. This is the substitutionary aspect of His death on Calvary. The blood of Jesus Christ was shed for us. He was our Substitute. We had no part in this phase of His death. This was entirely His work. But there was another aspect of His death in which we did have a part. The Scripture says that we were crucified with Christ, and "how shall we that are dead to sin, live any longer therein?" Or again, "So many of us as were baptized in Jesus Christ were baptized into His death." This, however, was not death "for" sin, but death "to" sin. When Christ died to sin, we died with Him.

The victory gained at Calvary over our foes is complete. Satan's power was broken (Heb. 2:14,15; Col. 2:15), and we were delivered from the world (Gal. 6:14). There is no weapon formed against us that can prosper. All our enemies were defeated at the cross. It is up to us to lay hold of that victory by faith in our daily experience. We must count it as true, and God will make it effective through the Holy Spirit.

Reckoning Made Real

When did Christ's death become effective for me? The moment I believed in Christ, the moment I, by faith, received Him as my Saviour. When does this death become effective in my behavior? The moment I reckon it so in my daily experience.

Let me raise another question. Cannot my crucifixion with Christ be tomorrow or some other day in the future? Perhaps you think that is a foolish question since the Scripture is so plain in telling us that we were crucified with Christ. Yet that is the way some believers look at the subject. They are still waiting to die to sin. My victory as a believer does not consist in looking forward to dying with Christ, but in accepting the fact that I died with Him more than 1900 years ago. God said that is so and that settles it. I cannot go by feelings or experience or anything other than the Word of God. The effect of that fact begins its work in us at the time we are born again.

A question some might well ask (because this is what they practice), is, "If I exert a great deal of effort, will I then be dead to sin?" No, no more than working for salvation saves anyone. In order to be saved, one must believe that Jesus completed the work of redemption. Equally so, it is only when a person accepts the finished work of Christ as true for himself that it becomes effectual in his life. What we must do is believe that Jesus Christ died to sin and that we died with Him, for in this way the power and claim of sin upon us was broken. To believe that as a simple fact will bring it into operation in our experience. God's way is so different from man's way. Some men advocate suppressing sin. Others want to eradicate sin, only to find out that it is still with them.

"But," someone asks, "if I am dead to sin why is it that I meet up with it so much?" The answer is simply this: Sin did not die. It is you who are to reckon yourself dead to sin, but not to reckon sin dead. This is a vital distinction.

Another illustration from the experience of Israel will help us here. We have already been reminded that God took Israel through the Red Sea in safety and destroyed Egypt's military might at the same time. What had God really done in this? He broke the power and grip of Egypt upon Israel so that while the nation of Egypt still existed, it could no longer enslave God's people by use of force. The only way the Israelites could become or remain slaves to the Egyptians was for the Hebrew nation to deliberately go back into Egypt and voluntarily come under the yoke of that nation again.

This is the only way a Christian can continue to be a slave to sin. He must deliberately say, "I still want to be a slave to sin and yield myself to it instead of yielding to God."

The secret of the victory which God gives us is in the fact that He has separated us from the claims and the power of sin. Such a truth cannot originate in the human mind; it comes to us only through divine revelation (Eph. 1:17,18). God will make this glorious fact plain to us if we give Him opportunity to do so. Ask the Holy Spirit to reveal this truth to you. He will do so if you wait on Him.

The fact that we were crucified with Christ gets to the bottom of the sin problem. It is with this that we must reckon. Christians sometimes say that they want to die to sin and that they want to live the new resurrection life. But God says we *are* dead and our life *is* hid with Christ in God (Col. 3:3). This is true; this is what God wants us to believe. There are some things we do not get rid of until we strike them at their source. We could not eliminate the liquor problem by just confiscating all liquor now in existence. It would be necessary to destroy all the sources of liquor, whether legal or illegal, in order to destroy the liquor traffic at its roots. So it is with the matter of sin. Our crucifixion with Christ separates us from that which produces sin in us. The evil nature is not eradicated, but its power has been destroyed in us. The evil nature has been disarmed. This is something we must reckon as true.

In verse 11 there is a double aspect of reckoning. The words are, "Likewise reckon ye also yourselves to be dead indeed unto sin, but alive unto God through Jesus Christ our Lord." This means, then, that we are to count true, to conclude as a fact, that we personally are dead to sin, and, at the same time, that we personally are alive to God.

Some Vital Questions

Can the Christian undo the fact that he has been crucified with Christ? The answer is clear when we ask the following question: "Can we undo the fact that Christ was crucified?" Of course not! Men deny it but that does not change the fact. No more can we undo the fact that each believer was crucified with Christ. We may ignore it, or through unbelief deny it, but we cannot change the fact.

Another question some ask is, "Does my reckoning myself dead to sin make me dead to sin?" No, for you are already dead to sin whether you reckon yourself to be dead to sin or not. That was a transaction completed more than 1900 years ago.

When I accept it as a fact, the benefits of that transaction become apparent in my daily experience.

It is when we reckon on this fact that God can enter in and give us the strength we need to overcome sin. As long as we count on our own strength we will go down in defeat. The Lord will share His glory with no one, but when we turn to Him in faith believing, He will provide the power necessary for victory over sin.

We are easily caught off guard, especially when we are trusting in ourselves. The procedure to follow in such a case is to confess to the Lord that we have failed and believe Him for forgiveness (I John 1:9). But we must also look to Him to put into effect in our daily lives by the Holy Spirit the reality of our having been crucified with Christ. That is something He has to do; we cannot do it.

We must learn that the victory lies with God and depend upon Him to make it effective in our lives. We may stumble and fall as we seek to apply these principles, but remember that old motto that we learned when children: "If at first you don't succeed, try, try again." We will have plenty of opportunity for practice, for there will be no letup in the temptations that face us from day to day.

If we fail—remember God cannot fail—let us come before Him with confession, as has been pointed out before. Our failure may be due to a lack of faith, or perhaps we have interfered with God's plan. Whatever the reason, if there is failure, it is our failure—not God's.

God's instructions in such a case are found in I John 1:9 where He says, "If we confess our sins, he is faithful and just to forgive us our sins, and to cleanse us from all unrighteousness." So then, every time we fail, let us confess it to God. Look to Him for mercy and for strength, and keep on in His way. By following such a course, the Christian life will not always be a series of failures but it will contain more and more victories.

A study of the life of David will disclose that he kept coming back to God and asking for mercy. The words "mercy" and "trust" are two of the outstanding words in his life. This is especially clear in the Psalms he wrote. When we sin, let us come and confess it to God and believe that we are forgiven right then. God assures us of forgiveness—He says so in I John 1:9 and that settles it. Then let us lean on God when we take the next step, trusting Him for victory.

Reckoning on What Is True

That on which God has called us to reckon is something that is true. To reckon something to be true when it is not true, is foolishness. I might reckon my car were a Cadillac, but that would not make it a Cadillac. Taking it to a garage and asking a mechanic to fix it up like a Cadillac would still not make it a Cadillac. God is not asking us to reckon as true matters which are false. We were crucified with Christ when He died on Calvary some 1900 years ago. That is a fact and, when reckoned on in our everyday Christian experience, it provides the foundation for victory.

Knowing precedes reckoning. To practice reckoning without knowing is useless. It is not that I reckon myself to be dead and therefore I am dead. Instead of that, I see what God has done for me in Christ, namely, that I have died with Jesus; and this I accept as a fact, established and final. My reckoning is not toward a death that I must yet die; but, rather, I reckon upon a death that has already been accomplished. We must take this attitude of simple faith before God can do His work in us.

There is a very real sense in which the word "reckon" is another word for faith. In the first five chapters of Romans the word "faith" is used 26 times. The word "believe" is also used interchangeably with it. But when we come to chapter 6 we find the word "reckon."

Pray earnestly in your own private devotional time that God will open your spiritual eyes to see that you have already been crucified with the Lord Jesus Christ. A mere head knowledge of this is not enough. It is not enough to know it in the mind, it must also be known in the heart. Something is needed that goes beyond a mere theological knowledge; it must be something that becomes practical in our experience.

Pray also that God will make this truth effective in your daily life. This death that we speak of is actual. But so far as its effectiveness in our lives is concerned, it is only potential until we appropriate it for ourselves.

Memory Assignment:
Memorize Romans 6:11.

EXAMINATION

Circle the correct letter:

1. The word "reckon" means
   a. to know something as a fact.
   b. to count something as a fact.
   c. to hope something is a fact.
2. Reckoning carries the idea that
   a. we count as true in our lives what we know as facts.
   b. we count as true in our lives what we want to be true.
   c. we expect our striving to accomplish its goals.
3. When the Scripture tells us that Christ died for sin, it means
   a. He, as our Substitute, paid sin's penalty.
   b. He delivered us from the influence of sin.
   c. He died at the hands of sinful men.
4. Because of our identification with Christ in His death to sin
   a. Satan's and sin's power over us are broken.
   b. sin no longer affects us.
   c. we are able to strive to be better.
5. When does Christ's death become effective in my behavior?
   a. The moment I receive Christ as Saviour.
   b. The moment I attain genuine spirituality.
   c. The moment I reckon it so in daily experience.

True or False:

6. _____ My victory as a believer consists in looking forward to dying with Christ.
7. _____ We must reckon ourselves dead to sin, but not reckon that sin is dead.
8. _____ The secret of Christian victory is in the fact that God has separated us from the claims and the power of sin.
9. _____ The double aspect of reckoning mentioned in Romans 6:11, emphasizes that we are (1) to count ourselves dead to sin and (2) to count sin dead to us.
10. _____ A Christian is already dead to sin whether or not he reckons it so.

Complete the following.

11. Every time we fail we should _____ it to God, ask for mercy and strength, then press forward.

22

12. In I John 1:9, God assures us of _____ when we _____ our sin.

13. _____ precedes reckoning.

14. In a very real sense the word "reckon" means the same as the word _____.

15. The truth of Romans 6 must be known in the _____ as well as in the mind.

☐   I have memorized Romans 6:11.

unit 3

Yielding and Walking

What the Believer Must Yield

The third important word that comes before us in Romans 6 is the word "yield." In verses 12 and 13 we read, "Let not sin therefore reign in your mortal body, that ye should obey it in the lusts thereof. Neither yield ye your members as instruments of unrighteousness unto sin: but yield yourselves unto God, as those that are alive from the dead, and your members as instruments of righteousness unto God." This word "yield" is the same as the word translated "present" in Romans 12:1.

A helpful distinction is made between yielding to sin and yielding to God in the following translation of verse 13: "Stop habitually putting your members at the service of sin as weapons of unrighteousness, but by a once-for-all act, put yourselves at the service of God" (Wuest). From this we learn that the old habit of yielding to the sin nature is to be interrupted and broken by a once-for-all act of yielding to God. This is to be followed by an attitude of constantly yielding to God. This is the heaven-given method of day-by-day victory over sin. Now let us take a closer look at what is included in this.

First the negative side is given—"yield not to sin." This involves all of our members—our hands, our minds, our eyes, our ears, the different parts of our bodies, the visible ones and the invisible ones, such as our heart attitudes. We must not yield our members to sin. Our sinful nature needs our members for the practice of sin. When the temptation comes to yield one of these members to sin, we must reckon on the fact that we have died to it. When temptation comes we need to say: "I am dead to that temptation." At the same time there is a positive side to yielding and we need to look to God and say, "But, Lord, I am alive to You. I am at Your disposal. Here are my members for You to use."

I believe by faith that I have died with Jesus, and by faith I ask Him to take over when temptation comes. I accept by faith the fact that He will take over, and He does just that.

But someone objects, saying, "I have tried that, and it failed." If there is failure, then it is in us. And the thing to do is to confess it to God, and He will forgive. When sin comes to tempt us again, we can say, "I refuse to yield my members to this temptation, but, Lord; I yield them to You, that You might use them in the way You want to."

We cannot control our thoughts without God's help, but we find that His weapons are adequate for our defense. Our every thought can be made subject to Christ: "(For the weapons of our warfare are not carnal, but mighty through God to the pulling down of strong holds;) Casting down imaginations, and every high thing that exalteth itself against the knowledge of God, and bringing into captivity every thought to the obedience of Christ" (II Cor. 10:4,5). What a remarkable promise this is for a day in which "brainwashing" is a common expression and which indicates unusual assaults being made upon the minds of men.

We turn to God when the wrong thoughts come and tell Him that we are trusting Him to take charge, and He does. It is not enough, however, to have the evil thought expelled; there must be something good to take its place. You have heard it said that nature abhors a vacuum, and that is true in the moral and spiritual realm just as well as in the physical world. For that reason, we should ask the Lord to give us the kind of thoughts He wants us to think when we ask Him to expel evil thoughts. Perhaps He will bring a Scripture passage to mind or some phase of service that He wants us to perform; but whatever it is, that vacuum must be filled. It will only be filled as we yield ourselves to God.

A key passage on what thoughts should fill our minds is Philippians 4:8: "Finally, brethren, whatsoever things are true, whatsoever things are honest, whatsoever things are just, whatsoever things are pure, whatsoever things are lovely, whatsoever things are of good report; if there be any virtue, and if there be any praise, think on these things."

The word "true" refers to sincerity in word. "Honest" has to do with action that is worthy of honor and respect. It is a word which one authority says "points to seriousness of purpose and to self-respect in conduct." The word "pure" comes from a word meaning holy. Its use in this passage suggests thoughts that are free from defilement, thoughts uncontaminated by sin.

The word "lovely" is not speaking of physical appearance but of character that is "lovable." It is describing conduct that is praiseworthy in the presence of others. On the other hand, "of good report" has reference to things we hear about others. It deals with conduct that is winning and gracious.

These are things with which our thoughts should be engaged whenever possible. We have to think about our work and our responsibilities in life, but there are many moments throughout the day and sometimes into the night when our minds are free to think of other things. Then it is that our thoughts should center in these matters.

If we pursue this a little farther and personify these qualities, we will find that they all point us to Christ himself. He is the honest and true One. He is pure, there is no defilement in Him. Who was ever found to be more lovable than He? There has never been His equal for graciousness in conduct and speech; and this found no better manifestation than at the time of His suffering and death. So let us fill our minds with these good things, and above all, let us center our thoughts on Christ, remembering as the Scripture exhorts us, to look "away unto Jesus, the author and the finisher of our faith" (Heb. 12:2).

Basic to the yielding of our body is this yielding of ourselves. We are to be given completely over to the Lord. Then, as it says in Romans 6, we are to yield our members; or, as it is expressed in Romans 12:1, we are to present our bodies.

The soul is that part of a person which we cannot see. We see the body in which he lives, but we do not see the actual person himself. We see his actions, and we can tell what kind of person he is by the way he lives. If he is a person who loses his temper often or speaks evil words, we know from that what is in his heart. But if God has complete control of a life, there will be words of love and compassion flowing from that body because God is in control of the soul. It goes without saying that if the members of my body are under God's control, I am under His control.

My own burden of prayer many mornings when I arise is, "Lord, I am dead to sin. I realize that to be a fact, but I cannot control my body, but I trust you to do so. I place myself at your disposal so that you can do your thinking and your acting through me. You can hear through me; you can speak through me; whatever it is you want, I am putting myself at your disposal."

The Believer's Walk

The fourth outstanding word to consider in Romans 6 is the word "walk." We are not only told to know certain truth, to reckon that truth to be true, and to yield ourselves to God, but we also are to walk—keeping all these factors in mind daily. Some may despair, believing that they have tried earnestly to walk with the Lord but have found themselves floundering. There is no reason to give up, but every reason to press ahead.

Paul had to depend on the Lord for victory just as we have to, and he said in Philippians: "I count all things but loss for the excellency of the knowledge of Christ Jesus my Lord: for whom I have suffered the loss of all things, and do count them but dung, that I may win Christ, And be found in him, not having mine own righteousness, which is of the law, but that which is through the faith of Christ, the righteousness which is of God by faith: That I may know him, and the power of his resurrection, and the fellowship of his sufferings, being made conformable unto his death; If by any means I might attain unto the resurrection of the dead. Not as though I had already attained, either were already perfect: but I follow after, if that I may apprehend that for which also I am apprehended of Christ Jesus" (3:8-12).

Paul denied any power in himself when he counted all but loss for Christ. And even though he lived a life that we are sure was well-pleasing to God, Paul knew he was not perfect. There were places where he failed, but he did not give up. He determined to go on, and this is what he meant when he said: "Brethren, I count not myself to have apprehended: but this one thing I do, forgetting those things which are behind, and reaching forth unto those things which are before, I press toward the mark for the prize of the high calling of God in Christ Jesus" (Phil. 3:13,14).

Paul did not want the death, burial and resurrection of Christ to be without effect in his daily life. He wanted to lay hold of that for which he had been laid hold of by God. In saying that he was forgetting those things which were behind, he did not mean he was overlooking his sins or failures. These were confessed to God according to the truth of I John 1:9, and then were left behind. He did not leave room for the Devil to throw those failures back at him. But if Satan did, then Paul pleaded the cleansing of the blood through Christ Jesus and reached forward to the things that lay before him. So we see that there is no reason for our going backward, but every reason to go forward. After our failures have been acknowledged and judged before God, let us leave them and go forward.

"Sin," Romans 6:14 tells us, "shall not have dominion over you: for ye are not under the law, but under grace." The Williams Translation makes this truth very emphatic: "For sin must not any longer exert its mastery over you, for now you are not living as slaves to law but as subjects to God's favor." All the law could say was, "Do this or die." It gave no power with which to perform its demands. It could condemn, but could not give life. On the other hand, grace enables us to please God for it is through grace that God does His work in and through us. The righteousness of God is produced in our lives as we yield ourselves to Him. The Spirit of God provides us the victory that is in Christ.

This portion of the Book of Romans does not describe the character of the believer's walk or conduct or manner of life, so much as it shows the method or the mechanics of victory in that walk. However, in Romans 6:4 the apostle says that the Christian "should walk in newness of life." This, of course, is the life made possible by the indwelling Christ and is in direct contrast to the old life in which the flesh nature ruled as king within.

By using the word "walk" as a guide in the epistles, we learn a good deal concerning the character of the believer's walk. It is to be an honest walk, one that is free from rioting and drunkenness, unmarred by unchastity, and without strife or envying (Rom. 13:13). It is a walk by faith and not by sight, which means that it is a walk in obedience to the Word of God (II Cor. 5:7;

Col. 2:6). It is to be a walk worthy of our calling, exhibiting lowliness of mind and meekness of spirit, an attitude of long-suffering with other believers in love (Eph. 4:1). This will make it a walk worthy of God (I Thess. 2:12).

That it is a walk in love and light and wisdom is emphasized in a number of Scriptures (Eph. 5:2,8,15; Col. 4:5; I John 1:6). It is all summed up as a walk in the Spirit and as walking as Christ walked. Concerning this God says through John the Apostle that He has no greater joy than to know that His children walk in truth (III John 3,4).

The new life in Christ not only breaks the shackles of sin but it produces in us the fruit and graces of the Holy Spirit.

Memory Assignment:
Memorize Romans 6:13.

EXAMINATION

True or False:
1. _____ We are told in Romans 6:12,13 to "let sin reign in your mortal body, that ye should obey it in the lust thereof."
2. _____ The expression "yield yourselves" in Romans 6:13 means the same as the expression in Romans 12:1, "present your bodies."
3. _____ The matter of yielding is not negative, it is only positive.
4. _____ Because the Christian still has the old nature within him, it is not possible for his every thought to be made subject to Christ.
5. _____ A Christian can maintain a healthy mental attitude by merely expelling every evil thought.

Circle the correct letter:

6. A key passage telling what thoughts should fill our minds is
   a. Philippians 1:8.
   b. Philippians 4:3.
   c. Philippians 4:8.

7. Thought patterns of the proper spiritual character
   a. come naturally after one accepts Christ as Saviour.
   b. are developed as one centers his thoughts on Christ.
   c. are developed through higher education.

8. The yielding of one's members (his body) to God is an indication of
   a. a partial surrender to God.
   b. a full surrender of his soul to God.
   c. a step toward the surrender of his life to God.

9. The four outstanding words of Romans 6 are "know," "reckon," "yield" and
   a. "trust."
   b. "walk."
   c. "obey."

10. When Paul said, "Forgetting those things which are behind," he meant
    a. he was trying to overlook his sins and failures.
    b. he was turning his back on lessons learned in the past.
    c. he had confessed his sins and failures and left them behind.

Complete the following.

11. While God's law can condemn us, only God's _____ can enable us to please Him.

12. Romans 6:4 says the Christian should walk in _____ of _____.

13. The walk of the Christian is by _____, not by sight.

14. The walk of the Christian may be summed up as a walk in the _____ and a walk as _____ walked.

15. The life in Christ breaks the shackles of sin and produces in us the _____ of the Holy Spirit.

☐ I have memorized Romans 6:13.

30

unit 4

Delivered From the Law

The seventh chapter of Romans seems to many to be a portion dealing with the confusion of a soul. For that very reason many wonder why the experience related in chapter 7 follows chapter 6 in which the Christian learns that he is dead, buried and raised with Jesus Christ. They cannot see the logic of following the truth that we are dead to sin and alive to God with an experience which shows a person going down in defeat. Some even say that chapter 7 should be where chapter 5 is.

We will find, however, that chapter 7 is in the right place. It explains experiences that all of us have had after learning the doctrinal truth of Romans 6. We determine, in gratitude to our Lord, that we are going to give ourselves wholeheartedly to Him because He has done so much for us. We set ourselves to serve Him with all our hearts only to find that we have difficulties to meet which we did not realize before. We find ourselves doing the very things we do not want to do, and the things we want to do we do not do. Like the apostle, "The good that I would I do not: and the evil which I would not, that I do." We wonder then at the confusion in which we find ourselves.

On the other hand there are some Christians who, when you ask them how they are getting along in their Christian life, will answer, "Well, I am still living in Romans 7. I haven't gotten over to Romans 8 yet." We recognize, of course, that Romans 8 deals with victory in the Christian life, and it is a great victory. It is necessary then, in view of the different approaches taken to Romans 7, that we learn the true practical aspect of this chapter as it relates to our Christian lives.

Paul uses a rather peculiar illustration here, in that he tells of a woman who, though married to one man, would like to be married to another.

The name of the man to whom she is married is "Law." He is a very exacting person who must have everything just so. His demands are right, for he is a good man, and his demands are good. But his demands are such that his wife just cannot begin to fulfill them. He lays certain requirements upon her, but gives her no power and makes no provision for her to meet them.

She sees another Man, and this Man's name is "Christ." Christ himself is perfect and the life He endorses is perfect, but unlike the Law He does not say, "Do this"; but He says, "Let Me do this in you, and let Me do it through you. This is what I want done, but I will do it." And this woman says that this is the kind of a man she wants to be married to; but she is tied to the man called "Law."

Now, the Law will never pass away. Every jot and tittle of it will be fulfilled. If the Law were to die, she, of course, would be free from her husband, but the Law never dies. What then can be done? What way of escape is there for her? Must she be under the authority of this first husband all the time?

Here is the illustration as Paul gives it to us: "Know ye not, brethren, (for I speak to them that know the law,) how that the law hath dominion over a man as long as he liveth? For the woman which hath an husband is bound by the law to her husband so long as he liveth; but if the husband be dead, she is loosed from the law of her husband. So then if, while her husband liveth, she be married to another man, she shall be called an adulteress: but if her husband be dead, she is free from that law; so that she is no adulteress, though she be married to another man. Wherefore, my brethren, ye also are become dead to the law by the body of Christ; that ye should be married to another, even to him who is raised from the dead, that we should bring forth fruit unto God" (Rom. 7:1-4).

Paul uses the marriage relationship to illustrate what takes place in the life of every person who receives Christ as Saviour.

The woman represents the individual who is born into the world under the condemnation of the Law (the first husband). The only way she can escape the sentence of the Law is to receive

Christ as Saviour (the second husband). When she receives Christ as Saviour she becomes "dead to the law by the body of Christ" (v. 4). Having died, the Law cannot exercise control over her any longer.

The Believer and the Law

It is strange that we should find so many Christian people who refuse this freedom from the bondage of the Law. Apparently they believe they can improve on God's message as evidenced by their desire to live under the Law, claiming they will keep it. Israel failed miserably under the Law. For 1500 years God proved man's inability to keep the Law. He did not give it that man might be saved by it, but to prove to men that they were sinners (Rom. 3:19,20). Anyone who claims that he can keep the Law does not have a proper knowledge about the purpose of the Law.

The Law exhibits and expounds God's law of righteousness, but gives no power to perform it. All it does is condemn us when we fail. God has set us free through Christ, both from the old Adamic nature and from the Law, that we might be free to live unto God.

The Law itself can never die. It is good, and God's demands in the Law can never be lowered. The Law makes me to see my sin, and condemns me because I am a sinner, but it does not help me to live a godly life. It is necessary, then, that my relationship to the Law be changed, and that is just exactly what takes place, I die, with Christ, to the Law. Sin no longer has dominion over us, because we have died with Christ. The Law no longer condemns us, and we are free from its curse. But God did not set us free from the Law in order that we might be free to sin. There are some people who believe that if we are free from the Law, then we will go into sin. They feel that the Law is that which keeps us from sinning. But they have missed entirely the point of the scriptural teaching. God frees us from the Law in order that He might live out His righteousness in us Himself.

Here is a man who is in prison. He has sinned against society, and is serving time for his crimes. Then, while in the penitentiary, he is saved. His whole life is changed. His attitude and behavior change while he is there. He begs to be released in order to prove that he can live a good life. His wish may not be granted right away, but his argument is sound, for he cannot prove that he can live that good life in prison. He does not have a society with its freedoms in which to exhibit his new life. He is hampered on every hand. He is held down. He is a prisoner. The Law does that for us, too. It holds us down and hampers us. It demands righteousness but gives us no strength to produce it. But in order for the prisoner to prove to the authorities and to society that Christ living in him will produce a righteous life through him, he is released from prison. Of course, he is watched. He is under parole, and is carefully checked on at regular intervals.

Now, why bring this illustration? Simply to show that this man was not released in order that he might continue to sin against society. He was given his release in order to prove that he was a changed man.

God has set us free, not only from the sin nature, but from the law of condemnation so that Christ can prove He lives a godly life in us. This we must see, because until this truth is understood, we will not have the proper attitude of faith with regard to Christ. If we feel we must live under the shadow of the Law all the time, we will live under condemnation all the time. No one who is conscious of being under the Law in this Biblical sense can live without the pressure of its condemnation.

Conviction and Condemnation

There is a difference between conviction and condemnation. When we do something wrong we often feel condemned. Conviction of sin is right. God has given us a conscience, and that conscience is for the purpose of bringing sin to our attention when we commit it. The conscience, when properly trained by the Word of God and under the control of the Holy Spirit, will convict us of our sin. That is right and proper, but Satan, the accuser of the brethren, comes along and holds the law over us, and condemns us for that evil thing. Then we try again, and again, and again to do the right thing—and find ourselves doing the wrong thing. The load of condemnation becomes heavier all the time. Finally, we get to the place where we excuse ourselves and say, "What's the use?" And that is when the Devil has us where he wants us. He wants us to get so tired of trying to live the godly life that we will give up in despair. Or he may want

34

us to justify ourselves and blame our evil deeds on our carnal nature.

Let me repeat that conviction is right, but condemnation is wrong. Satan would take us to Mt. Sinai, to the place of the Law, and condemn us. The Holy Spirit, on the other hand, takes us to Calvary, and to Jesus. Christ shows us the wounds in His hands and in His feet, the crown upon His head, the pierced side, the blood that was shed, and He says to us, "I anticipated every sin and every failure of yours, not only those that are past, but those of the present and the future. I have paid the price for every one of them. I ask you only to confess them (I John 1:9), and I will clear your record and will live in you, and live My life in you. But if you go back under the law, I cannot do one thing for you. But if you will come to Me at Calvary, I will forgive you."

But you say, "What if I do it again and again? Will He still hold out the hand of forgiveness?" He will, for He knows that in ourselves we are no good, and the sooner we find that out the better off we are (Rom. 7:18).

The problem in Romans 7 is that of a man who finds when he tries to do right, he does wrong, and of course the Law condemns him. Then he comes to the realization, as expressed in verse 18: "For I know that in me dwelleth no good thing." The Phillips Translation puts it thus: "(And indeed I know from experience that the carnal side of my being can scarcely be called the home of good!) I often find that I have the will to do good, but not the power. That is, I don't accomplish the good I set out to do, and the evil I don't really want to do I find I am always doing." That is the condition of any believer who seeks to live the Christian life apart from Christ living in him. It was because he was faced with this dilemma that Paul cried out, "O wretched man that I am! who shall deliver me from the body of this death?"

The answer was already given in Romans 6:14, where the words are, "Sin shall not have dominion over you: for ye are not under the law, but under grace." Grace means that God gives us something that we do not deserve, because He wants to give it to us. Under Law, I try to do something for God, and fail. But under grace we find that Christ says, "I will come and do it for you." The Law requires something from me, but grace says, "The requirements are provided for us by Christ's presence in us."

In Romans 7 we find a man trying to do something for God, only to find that he is brought under condemnation by the Law because of his failure to do what he knows he ought to do. There is nothing wrong with the Law, for verse 12 says that the Law is holy, and just and good. The problem is not with the Law, it is with us.

The United States law requires that I pay a certain amount of tax. That is right and good. But if I were to dissipate my finances to where I could not meet the tax imposed on me, then I would be in difficulty. The law would be requiring far more than I was able to pay. It would expose my inability to meet the tax requirements. Suppose, however, that a friend would come along and say, "I have the means to meet the demands, and will pay your tax for you." Then my difficulty with the government would be ended.

Deliverance through Christ is very real, and very complete, for we read, "But now we are delivered from the law, that being dead wherein we were held; that we should serve in newness of spirit, and not in the oldness of the letter."

God allows us to pass through the experience related in Romans 7 in order to bring us to the end of ourselves. We come to learn the doctrinal truth as stated in Romans 6, and that is all wonderful and good. Then we find ourselves failing constantly in the Christian life, and we wonder why. God seemingly has to teach us the hard way. Most of us seem to have to learn that way, for it is not until we despair of our own efforts that we are willing to allow God to work in and through us. Moreover, we need to remember that just because we are dead to the Law and dead to sin, this does not mean that there will be no more temptation. Sin itself is not dead. It is we who are dead to it. That does not mean that it cannot come along and tempt us, but when it does, we can turn to the Lord saying, "Lord, I am dead to that, please take over quickly and deliver me." Some Christians are tempted even more because Satan gets on the rampage, knowing that these Christians have come to a new knowledge of truth, and he wants to overthrow them. But they will find Christ sufficient, as Paul did. Paul came to the end of himself and cried, "O wretched man that I am! who shall deliver me from the body of this death?" Do not stop here and give up in despair and say,

"What's the use?" Paul follows that sentence with these words: "I thank God through Jesus Christ our Lord." It is Jesus Christ who will deliver us, and this is the theme of Romans chapter 8.

Memory Assignment:
Memorize Romans 7:6.

EXAMINATION

True or False:

1. _____ Romans 7 should actually come before chapter 6 because of the experiences it describes.
2. _____ Paul's summary of his problem is, "The good that I would I do: and the evil which I would not, that I do not do."
3. _____ The illustration in Romans 7:1-4 makes it plain that one can be freed from the Law only by being dead to it.
4. _____ The demands of Christ are right and good, but He makes no provision for a person to keep His demands.
5. _____ The woman in Romans 7:1-4 represents the person under the condemnation of the Law who can escape the sentence only by keeping the Law to the letter.

Complete the following.

6. God gave the Law to prove that men were _____.
7. Christians are freed from the Law in order that _____ might live out His righteousness in them.
8. No one who is conscious of being under the Law in the biblical sense can live without its _____.
9. _____ of sin is right; but _____ is wrong.
10. The problem of Romans 7 is that of a man who does _____ when he tries to be right.

Circle the correct letter:
11. Any believer who seeks to live the Christian life apart from Christ living in him must describe his experience thus:
    a. "I have victory when I sincerely try to live on a spiritual plane."
    b. "I have more victory as I gain experience in the Christian life."
    c. "I don't accomplish the good I set out to do, and I find I am always doing the evil I don't really want to do."
12. Under law I try to do something for God, and fail; but under grace Christ says,
    a. "I will help you keep the law."
    b. "I will come and do it for you."
    c. "You are free to live as you please."
13. God allows us to pass through the experience related in Romans 7 in order to
    a. bring us to the end of ourselves.
    b. bring us to despair.
    c. tempt us.
14. The Christian's relationship to sin may be stated thus:
    a. Sin itself is dead to the Christian.
    b. The Christian cannot sin.
    c. The Christian is dead to sin.
15. Paul follows his cry, "O wretched man that I am," with the statement,
    a. "There is no deliverance from the body of this death."
    b. "Who shall deliver me from the body of this death?"
    c. "There is hope for deliverance if I keep struggling."

☐ I have memorized Romans 7:6.

unit 5

One Step at a Time

A New Life Principle

The first thing we learn in Romans 8 is that "There is therefore now no condemnation to them which are in Christ Jesus." The reason for such a statement is that the Law comes along and condemns us saying, "You have not done what you ought to do." But God declares that there is no condemnation to those of us who are in Christ Jesus. It matters not what the Law says—it cannot condemn us any more. Why? Because Jesus has already taken that condemnation.

But what about the sin that has been committed? We must confess it. There must be the confession that we have sinned, and have failed, and have broken our fellowship (I John 1:9). But we are not condemned. Convicted, yes, but not condemned. This we must believe or we will never grow spiritually.

There is no deliverance in ourselves, but God makes deliverance available through Himself. In effect, God says to sin: "You have no right to this man. I am going to give him power and I am going to be the power in him, for I will live in him and will overcome sin in him." Paul says, "The law of the Spirit of life in Christ Jesus hath made me free from the law of sin and death."

The law of gravity holds me down so that I cannot fly to the moon by myself. In order to reach that goal another law would have to intervene, a law stronger than gravity. So it is in the Christian life. The law of sin and death is overcome by the much more powerful spirit of life in Christ Jesus, and I am enabled to overcome sin.

The first four verses of Romans 8 read: "There is therefore now no condemnation to them which are in Christ Jesus, who walk not after the flesh, but after the Spirit. For the law of the Spirit of life in Christ Jesus hath made me free from the law of sin and death. For what the law could not do, in that it was weak through the flesh, God sending his own Son in the likeness of sinful flesh, and for sin, condemned sin in the flesh: That the righteousness of the law might be fulfilled in us, who walk not after the flesh, but after the Spirit."

Two Laws or Principles

The phrase, "the law of Christ," is often used. In this passage it is "the law of the Spirit of life in Christ Jesus." Some may wonder just what the difference is between the law of Christ and the Old Testament Law. The law of Christ is simply the life which God wants to see worked out in us. The word "law" does not *always* mean a written law, such as the Ten Commandments, or such as we have with regard to our state or federal governments. The word is also used to mean a principle, just as the law of gravity is a principle. The law of Christ is a basic principle of life for the believer.

Jesus Christ died for all our sins—past, present and future. All our sins were future when He died. We were not yet born, and consequently, had not committed any sins. They were all future, and Jesus died for all of them. Perhaps when we accepted Christ as our Saviour we did not realize how complete the salvation was that God had provided for us. But it is there, covering all our sins—past, present and future. So far as condemnation is concerned, the Evil One may make us feel condemned, but we cannot really be condemned before God. Until we are willing to trust God for this we cannot go on.

Romans 8:2 says, "For the law of the Spirit of life in Christ Jesus hath made me free from the law of sin and death." We have already seen that this law is in reality a principle. It is not a commandment in the sense of an Old Testament commandment. Furthermore, the law of the Spirit of life is also known as the "law of Christ." This is Christ, through the Holy Spirit, forming His life in us. The law of sin and death is the principle of law found in the Old Testament, in the Gospels and in the Epistles. It is the law that points out sin to be sin. The law was given to show that man is a sinner, and to stop every mouth from boasting.

If there were no speed law, a person could travel at any speed he desires and he would not be breaking any speed law. But if a speed limit is established, a person goes against the law when he travels faster than that speed. Such a person is subject to and deserves a fine. So God gave the Law to identify sin, and to show man that because he could not keep the Law he deserved death. The wages of sin is death. A person who fails in one point of the Law is guilty of all, for to break one law is to be guilty of breaking all the Law (James 2:10). The penalty, from which there is no escape except through Christ, is death. It is for this reason that the Apostle identifies the Law as the law of sin and death.

Weak Through the Flesh

The law of the Spirit of life in Christ Jesus has made me free from this law of sin and death. Romans 8:3,4 explains the reason for this: "For what the law could not do, in that it was weak through the flesh, God sending his own Son in the likeness of sinful flesh, and for sin, condemned sin in the flesh: That the righteousness of the law might be fulfilled in us, who walk not after the flesh, but after the Spirit." The Law could not produce righteousness in us; it could only condemn us for our lack of righteousness. This, of course, brought us to see our own sinfulness. The tendency in man is to be proud of his own goodness, and God had to bring him to a realization of his sinfulness. But the Law could not produce the righteous life in man that God wants. The Law itself is good, but its righteous demands could not be met by the flesh. Christ was the only One who had the power to fulfill the Law. It was not weak in Him, but it is weak in us.

God sent His only begotten Son in the likeness of sinful flesh, that He might take care of the sin that we have committed. Christ came not only to deliver us from the penalty of sin, but also to be the power within us through which the righteousness of the Law could be fulfilled.

Christ, in His work on Calvary, made provision for our victory over sin by breaking sin's power. He condemned sin in the flesh, and thus sin lost its death-grip on us. The sin nature was left judged and dethroned, and its power over us was broken like that of an exiled dictator who, though still alive, is separated from his country and has no say or power in its government.

The New Walk in Christ

Another important word is found in Romans 8:4—"walk." The Law will be fulfilled in us who do not walk after the flesh but after the Holy Spirit. The actual method God uses is that Christ indwells us and lives in and through us.

This phase of the Christian life has been much misunderstood by God's people. We treat God as though He were a medicine chest to which we come for a pill for our need.

But God does not dispense the various graces. He has only one Gift for us, and that Gift is the Lord Jesus Christ himself. He is our life, and He lives in us. Consequently, if it is patience we need, God does not give us patience, but He teaches us to turn to Christ, and to let Him be the patience in us. If it is humility we need, then we are to turn to Jesus, recognizing that He is the Vine, and that we are the branches. All the life is in Him. Humility lies in Him and it is expressed only to the degree that we permit Christ to live His life in us.

One Step at a Time

Now, as to the outworking of this life, we must realize that we take one step at a time. That is where this word "walk" begins to take on real significance. That is the way small children learn. They take the first step, then they stop and think, and finally take a second step. After a while they can walk a little better, and soon they begin to run.

The dictionary definition for the word "walk" is to advance by steps, lifting one foot while the other is securely on the ground. This is different than running. When a person runs, both feet are in the air part of the time. But in walking, we never take another step until we have securely planted one foot on solid ground, then we take the next step. It is well to keep this in mind, as we discuss this matter of walking in the spiritual life.

The word "walk" can also be defined to mean the pursuing of a course of life, or the manner in which one conducts himself. It is a word which describes behavior, and it is with this meaning that the word is employed quite often in the Bible. The believer's walk includes the whole round of his activities as an individual. There is a related Bible meaning which is also very vital. "Walk" also means the keeping in step with another with submission of heart to that other who is the Holy Spirit.

Many passages in the Bible speak of the walk of the Christian, both instructing how he should walk and how he should not walk.

A Walk of Faith

Keep in mind that walking in the spiritual sense is a walk of faith. We must not become discouraged if we do not walk at first as mature Christians or are not able to run the race as we should. We grow in grace and in the knowledge of our Saviour, Jesus Christ.

It may be that we see some desirable goal in the spiritual life. How do we attain to it? We depend upon the Holy Spirit to lead us step by step and give us the power to move in the right direction.

Perhaps it is a financial matter that faces us. Perhaps we will not take a step with God until a full financial provision has been made. God says that we are to walk by faith—one step at a time. How easy it really is. It is a walk for which God makes constant provision.

We have seen that salvation in Christ includes victory over sin. The first step in making this victory effective in our daily experience is coming to know that we are identified with Christ in His death, burial and resurrection. On this we reckon, count it true, regard it as a fact, in our daily experience. We are also to completely yield our bodies to the Lord. We are then to walk in the power of the Holy Spirit; and as we walk in the Spirit, we will find that we do not fulfill the desires of the flesh nature.

Memory Assignment:
Memorize Romans 8:3.

EXAMINATION

Complete the following.

1. "There is therefore now no _____ to them which are in Christ Jesus."

2. The law of sin and death is overcome by the much more powerful _____ _____ _____ in Christ Jesus.

3. The law of Christ is a basic _____ of life for the believer.

4. The penalty of the Law, from which there is no escape except through Christ, is _____.

5. Because the Law could not produce righteousness in us, it was described as being weak through the _____.

True or False:

6. ____ Christ came to be the power within us through which the righteousness of the Law could be fulfilled.

7. ____ Sin lost its death-grip on us because Christ, at Calvary, made provision for our victory over sin.

8. ____ The Law will be fulfilled in those who walk after the flesh.

9. ____ God dispenses various graces according to the Christian's needs.

10. ____ All aspects of spiritual life are found in the indwelling life of Christ.

Circle the correct letter.

11. The dictionary definition for the word "walk" is
    a. to advance by steps.
    b. to move forward quickly.
    c. to move in a sliding fashion.

12. The believer's walk, as described in Scripture, includes:
    a. his devotional life primarily.
    b. only his relationship to the world.
    c. all his activities.

13. The Christian's walk is a walk
    a. by faith and by sight.
    b. by sight.
    c. by faith.
14. To obtain a desirable goal in the spiritual life, the Christian should
    a. depend upon the Holy Spirit to lead him step by step.
    b. strive toward the goal with all his strength.
    c. move forward as quickly as possible.
15. The proper order of steps in making victory effective in daily experience is:
    a. reckon, know, yield, walk.
    b. yield, reckon, know, walk.
    c. know, reckon, yield, walk.

☐ I have memorized Romans 8:3.

unit 6

The Key to Victory

Romans 8:13 might well be described as the key to the victorious Christian life: "For if ye live after the flesh, ye shall die: but if ye through the Spirit do mortify the deeds of the body, ye shall live." God's purpose in giving us such a verse is to point us to the way of victory. It is possible, however, for us to feel frustrated by such a declaration, or to allow ourselves to be brought under condemnation by it. Such has been the reaction of some of God's people to this truth; but there is absolutely no basis for such thinking. Just as there is no condemnation to those who are in Christ Jesus, there is absolutely no place for frustration among God's children. His plan and promise is for victory, and this verse shows us how.

This particular passage says nothing about our losing our salvation or about gaining salvation on the basis of mortifying the deeds of the flesh. If it did, it would contradict the truth laid down in Romans 3-5 that we are saved on the basis of justification in Christ Jesus and not on the basis of human works or merit. Consequently, since justification is a once-for-all work, whatever this passage in Romans 8 teaches it will not contradict any previous doctrine laid down in the same book or anywhere else in the Word of God.

There are several matters that must be kept clearly in mind if we would see the truth involved in Romans 8:13. First of all, a Christian's body is the temple of the Holy Spirit. Secondly, there are two natures that at present live in that body—the old sinful nature which we as members of the human race inherit at birth, and the divine nature which we who trust in Christ received at the new birth. Through the new birth I became identified with Christ, so that this new nature is Christ in me. Christ and I together constitute the new man. He is the life and the power, and I am united with Him.

A Faith Walk

It is evident, then, that only because of the presence and power of the Holy Spirit within him, the believer may have his mind renewed and his will made submissive to the will of God. If we walk after the Spirit we will not fulfill the desires of the flesh. This is a "by faith" walk. Christ is in us; He is in control, but it is our responsibility to submit to Him.

A clear illustration of this is given in the first chapter of James: "Let no man say when he is tempted, I am tempted of God: for God cannot be tempted with evil, neither tempteth he any man [to do evil]: But every man is tempted, when he is drawn away of his own lust [the desires of the old nature], and enticed. Then when lust hath conceived, it bringeth forth sin; and sin, when it is finished, bringeth forth death." First comes temptation to do evil. This temptation comes from the old nature, or it may have its source in Satan or the world who work through the evil nature. I am united to Christ, but I have charge of my body and my mind. When my mind becomes aware of a particular temptation, what do I do? How I react makes all the difference in the world. If the temptation comes from the old nature, whether or not Satan or the world is back of it, and I succumb to it, then I am guilty of sin.

God will never lend His power or influence or His Holy Spirit to help the flesh nature fulfill its desires.

What if we fail? We are told in I John 1:9: "If we confess our sins, he is faithful and just to forgive us our sins, and to cleanse us from all unrighteousness."

When we overcome temptation by yielding to the Holy Spirit, the fruit of the Spirit mentioned in Galatians 5:22,23 will be seen in our lives.

Children and Sons

The walk of the Christian is still before us in Romans 8:14-17: "For as many as are led by the Spirit of God, they are the

47

sons of God. For ye have not received the spirit of bondage again to fear; but ye have received the Spirit of adoption, whereby we cry, Abba, Father. The Spirit itself [Himself] beareth witness with our spirit, that we are the children of God: And if children, then heirs; heirs of God, and joint-heirs with Christ; if so be that we suffer with him, that we may be also glorified together."

Those who walk after the Spirit are the sons of God. It does not say, however, that we become the sons of God by being led by the Spirit. The subject here is not dealing with the beginning of salvation but with the results of it.

Two words are used in this passage which speak of family relationship, and though the words are similar in meaning, they are not identical. Verse 14 speaks of those led by the Spirit of God as being "sons" of God. In verse 16, however, we are described as "children" of God. In our everyday conversation, we make little or no distinction in these matters. For example, a man who has several sons might introduce them to someone and say, "These are my sons." Or he might just as correctly say, "These are my children." But in Paul's day there was a marked difference between these two words. The word "children" emphasizes our new birth and new life in Christ, but the word "sons" emphasizes the position given us in God's family.

In a Jewish household those who were under age were called "children," but those male children who had come of age were called "sons." As mature persons, they entered into the privileges which were rightfully theirs as members of the family. There were special ceremonies which were attached to this "son placing" in the Jewish home, for it was a very special time in the life of any young man.

The word "adoption" is also used in this connection and means "son placing." Paul uses the word in Romans 8:15-17, in Ephesians 1:5 and Galatians 4:4-6.

The Spirit of Adoption

Another great truth which we need to see is that we have "not received the spirit of bondage again to fear; but ye have received the Spirit of adoption, whereby we cry, Abba, Father" (Rom. 8: 15). As full-grown, mature sons, our conduct will be somewhat in contrast to that of children; and one of the things pointed out here is that we have not received the spirit of fear. This can be seen in our handling of sin. If we fail Him, we are to confess our failures and accept His forgiveness. Then, as full-grown sons, we are to cry: "Abba Father, I have failed you again, but forgive me" (I John 1:9).

Meaning of Adoption

The Bible use of the word "adoption" is not quite the same as the present-day meaning.

For example, we think of a childless couple who desire children and so adopt a child. It may be a boy who is adopted, taken into the home as a son, given the family name, and made the family heir. In this way, he is treated as a full-fledged son even though he is only an adopted child. This, of course, only partially pictures the scriptural teaching in this passage, for what we find is that in the spiritual realm God takes those who are already His children by the new birth and places them as full-fledged sons. We become the children of God by being born again, but we are called the sons of God when we accept our responsibility before God and allow the Holy Spirit to control us and lead us.

Discipline

The discipline for a child will be different from that of a mature son. A child may receive some kind of chastisement when he has failed because he is under the strict rule of his parents. But we need to reach the place in our spiritual lives where we recognize that God forgives when we confess and He treats us as full-grown sons.

Children by Birth

Verses 16 and 17 of Romans 8 emphasize that we are called the children of God. In doing so these verses remind us of our salvation through Christ. God does not want us in any way to feel that every time we fail Him as sons we must start the spiritual life all over again by being born again. There is no condemnation to them who are in Christ Jesus. Sin separates us in fellowship but not in relationship. The Spirit bears witness with our spirit that we are God's children.

How does the Spirit of God bear witness? It is not a matter of feeling. A person's outward appearance may show whether he is happy or sad, but that has nothing to do with the Spirit's witness. Bearing witness is done by means of the Word. The

Spirit of God bears witness to my spirit when He says, "He that heareth my word, and believeth on him that sent me, hath everlasting life, and shall not come into condemnation." He bears witness to that scriptural truth from which I cannot escape. He drives that truth home to me. He makes it so that I believe it because "faith cometh by hearing and hearing by the Word of God." But it takes the Holy Spirit to make the Word live within us.

When we are tempted to think that something cannot be true even though the Word of God assures us that it is true, let us take the position that since God has said it, that settles it.

Heirship and Suffering

Romans 8:14-17 also carries us from the thought of being children on to the fact that we are heirs. The word "if" in verse 17 is used with the meaning of "since." "Since we are the children of God" we are heirs of God. All that God has for us is ours by inheritance. We are heirs of Christ Jesus because we are united with Him, and all things are ours in Him. Because we are Christ's, and Christ belongs to the Father, and all things that belong to the Father are Christ's, then they are also ours. Now this means not only material things, but spiritual things also. This is further assured to us in Romans 8:32: "He that spared not his own Son, but delivered him up for us all, how shall he not with him also freely give us all things?"

Heirship and suffering go hand in hand, for this passage also says, "If so be that we suffer with him." Suffering is not confined to physical suffering. Any man who will go out and out for God will suffer in one way or another even at the hands of weaker Christians. Possibly some of the worst enemies Christians have today are not people of the world but backslidden believers.

We suffer with Him that we may also be glorified with Him. According to verse 30 of this same chapter, there is a sense in which we are glorified now. But so far as our experience is concerned, our glorification is something future. And all of this is ours because we are His. In the light of these facts, let us not be satisfied with merely being children of God, but let us grow until God can declare us to be full-grown, mature sons—those that the Holy Spirit controls and fills.

Suffering as a joint-heir with Christ is in some way or another the result of sin. This does not mean a person who suffers has committed some sin of His own and is thereby suffering for it, but that suffering in general is the result of sin being in the world. Jesus came, partook of flesh and blood and also of man's sufferings, not because He sinned, but because of man's sin.

Deliverance From Corruption

More light on the blessings ahead is given in the next verses in Romans where the words are: "For the earnest expectation of the creature waiteth for the manifestation of the sons of God. For the creature was made subject to vanity, not willingly, but by reason of him who hath subjected the same in hope. Because the creature itself also shall be delivered from the bondage of corruption into the glorious liberty of the children of God. For we know that the whole creation groaneth and travaileth in pain together until now" (Rom. 8:19-22).

According to this statement, everything in nature is in the bondage of corruption. It is all in a state of death whether it be plant life, animal kingdom or man. All around is death and decay. Because man sinned, all of creation was put into this state of bondage, not of its own will, but because in the wisdom of God, such was best for it.

There is a time coming when creation will be delivered from its past corruption. We believe this will be seen in the millennial age. There will still be death during that time, but not to the extent we see it now. The plant and animal kingdoms will thrive as they have not done since the time of Eden.

Present Deliverance

In verse 21 there is indicated a partial deliverance for the children of God even now. The verse reads: "Because the creature itself also shall be delivered from the bondage of corruption into the glorious liberty of the children of God." This suggests that already, by the Holy Spirit, there has been given us an earnest of the liberty which will be completely ours in the future. We are given liberty sufficient to live victoriously. We shall live in a corruptible body, but someday that corruptible body shall put on incorruption and in a moment—in a twinkling of an eye —it shall be changed. That is the glorious anticipation of what will take place when we meet the Lord in the air. At present, we groan within ourselves waiting for the redemption of our body, and such redemption will be the final step in our adoption. Our ultimate placing as sons will occur when we receive the new body in which we will no longer be susceptible to sin.

We have already pointed out that liberty to live victoriously is ours now. In writing to the Galatians, Paul said, "Stand fast therefore in the liberty wherewith Christ hath made us free, and be not entangled again with the yoke of bondage" (Gal. 5:1). Man was put under the yoke of bondage because of His sin. But Jesus Christ paid for that sin. Not only that, He put aside the law which kept men under bondage by fulfilling that law Himself. He now lives in us, thus making it possible for us to fulfill the righteous requirements of the law.

Our obligation is to stand fast in our liberty. We have been released from what would naturally hold us down. Some believers may say they cannot live a godly life, but they have no right to say such a thing. By so doing they deny that God says we have liberty to live victoriously.

Liberty does not give us liberty to sin. Paul says, "For, brethren, ye have been called to liberty; but use not liberty for an occasion to the flesh, but by love serve one another." The law itself is fulfilled in love, and this love has been placed in our hearts by God.

Memory Assignment:
Memorize Romans 8:13.

EXAMINATION

Complete the following.

1. "For if ye live after the flesh, ye shall _____: but if ye through the Spirit do mortify the deeds of the body, ye shall _____."

2. A Christian's body is the _____ of the _____ _____.

3. The Christian has with him two natures—the _____ and the _____.

4. Christ is in us; He is in control, but it is our responsibility to _____ to Him.

5. Three sources from which temptation come are: _____ _____, _____ and _____.

Circle the correct letter:

6. When we confess our sins, God has said
   a. we must also do penance.
   b. He will punish and forgive us.
   c. He will forgive and cleanse us.

7. The expression "sons of God" in Romans 8:14 emphasizes
   a. our new birth.
   b. our new life in Christ.
   c. our position in God's family.

8. As sons of God, we have received the
   a. Spirit of fear.
   b. Spirit of adoption.
   c. Spirit of bondage.

9. In bearing witness that we are God's children, the Holy Spirit deals through
   a. our feelings.
   b. circumstances around us.
   c. God's Word.

10. Believers are heirs of God, and joint-heirs with Christ because
    a. they are united with Christ.
    b. they strive to please God.
    c. they deserve all God has for them.

True or False:
11. _____ Suffering goes hand in hand with being an heir of God.
12. _____ Everything in nature is in a state of death.
13. _____ The redemption of our body will take place when the Lord Jesus returns.
14. _____ Our new bodies will not be subject to sin.
15. _____ The liberty given to Christians does not give them liberty to sin.

☐ I have memorized Romans 8:13.

unit 7

The Interceding Holy Spirit

We who have trusted in Christ are not left without a helper. Jesus promised His disciples that He would send the Holy Spirit to them. He would go alongside of them, stand by them and be a Comforter in them. In Romans 8 we read, "Likewise the Spirit also helpeth our infirmities: for we know not what we should pray for as we ought: but the Spirit itself maketh intercession for us with groanings which cannot be uttered" (v. 26).

The word "infirmities" means "weaknesses"—general weaknesses. The world is full of such, for we are told that the whole creation "groaneth and travaileth in pain together until now." But this is not limited to one segment of creation, because we who are believers "which have the firstfruits of the Spirit, even we ourselves groan within ourselves, waiting for the adoption, to wit, the redemption of our body."

The world has always been full of tests and trials for the believer, and in our time these are, without question, on the increase. The whole world is living in fear of war. The Christian has to live in this environment of fear and worry which characterizes the world. Coupled with that there is also our own helplessness. Seemingly we cannot do what we want to do; we cannot even pray as we ought to pray; but, in the midst of it all, God gives us this wonderful assurance—the Spirit helps us in our weaknesses.

We have many weaknesses even in our prayer life. In this area we are helped in two ways: What we should pray for and how we ought to pray. We have difficulties in both realms and the Spirit promises to help us with them.

The intercession of the Holy Spirit is not made in heaven. Intercession before God in heaven is made for us by Christ who is at the right hand of the Father. The Spirit of God, on the other hand, makes intercession for us from within us. And the groanings of which Scripture speaks are the yearnings which we cannot express because of our weaknesses.

The Spirit's Desire

The statement, "The Spirit itself [Himself] maketh intercession for us with groanings which cannot be uttered," is phrased thus by one translator: "His compassion matches our yearnings." That is a good translation. His compassion for us, His desire to see that we have the best from God, that we pray according to the will of God, is such that He inspires that kind of prayer with us. But His compassion not only matches our yearnings, He also raises our desires to higher and holier levels than human language can express. There are sighs and longings within us that human words cannot say. Sometimes we do not pray in public because we are afraid we cannot find the right words to use. We need the help of the Holy Spirit to enable us to express the real longings of our hearts.

The 27th verse continues the subject of the Spirit's intercession: "And he that searcheth the hearts knoweth what is the mind of the Spirit, because he maketh intercession for the saints according to the will of God." Since it is God the Son who makes intercession for us in heaven, it is possibly He who is spoken of here as searching the hearts. There is complete understanding between the Holy Spirit in us and the Lord Jesus Christ at the right hand of God the Father. Christ knows what the Spirit means even though we cannot put it into human words. This should encourage us not to be afraid of praying just because we cannot phrase our prayers as well as some do. Christ looks to see what the Spirit of God is doing in our souls, for that is all important.

God's Goal for the Believer

"We know that all things work together for good to them that love God, to them who are the called according to his purpose" (8:28). These are glorious words whose meaning is expanded and clarified by what follows in the chapter.

Consider Romans 8:28 and James 4:6-8 together. These passages speak of the same truth though the approach is different. In the latter we read, "But he giveth more grace. Wherefore he saith, God resisteth the proud, but giveth grace unto the humble. Submit yourselves therefore to God. Resist the devil, and he will flee from you. Draw nigh to God, and he will draw nigh to you" (James 4:6-8). Romans 8:28 tells us that all things work together for good to them that love God. At the same time we gather from this Scripture that the testings which are part of the "all things" may come either from God or from the Devil. But regardless of the source, if we submit ourselves to God—and it is the humble person who will do so—then God will give us more grace.

God never allows anything to come into our lives that is going to harm us spiritually. God cannot tempt us with evil, for such would be contrary to His own character. When God permits a testing to come to us, He has nothing wrong in mind for us, but only good. Even if Satan brings a testing, God has permitted it and has promised to give more grace and also a way of escape.

God is talking in Romans 8:28 to Christians who have accepted their maturity in Christ. They know the doctrine of Romans 6 and have put it into practice for victorious lives, according to Romans 8. But God does not say that sin works together for good in us. That, we believe, is excluded from this verse. The testings and trials and problems of this life are not sin. Deliberate sin is most certainly excluded.

Working Together

The word "together" in Romans 8:28 is very significant. There are many things that come into our lives which, if we consider them separately, we cannot see any benefit from them. Of course, a raise in salary, or a bumper crop present no difficulties to us in this respect. But when a hail storm destroys part or all of the crop or there is sickness in the home or work gets slack, we cannot always see how such things can work together for good. The ingredients that go into the making of a cake would not all be palatable by themselves, but when all are mixed together properly and the cake is baked, the result can be delicious. So it is with the "all things" in our lives.

God's Foreknowledge

The next verses throw further light on the 28th verse. The 29th verse begins, "For whom he did foreknow, he also did predestinate." The word "foreknowledge" gives some people a good deal of trouble because they try to think of God as being bound to thinking as we do. There are actually very few things that any of us really foreknow to any degree. We can look at the past and see the past. We can view the present and realize what is happening today, but most of the future we cannot foreknow. We are all creatures of time and are limited in our knowledge with regard to what lies ahead.

This, however, is no problem to God. He knows what is in the future. But what to us may seem more remarkable, to Him everything is present. You and I do not understand how that can be, but we do not have to understand it, only know it and believe it. Before the foundation of the world you and I were already present with God in His heart and mind. Away in the far distant past my life and your life was open to God as though it were being lived before Him then. Our whole life was outlined according to His plan, and He knew just what each one of us would do. God always sees the end as well as the beginning.

What foreknowledge can mean and how it may operate for good can be dimly seen in the following illustration. Suppose there is a farmer who has many head of cattle and most of his farm is on low ground by a river. A warning is suddenly given to him that the river is rising and in 24 hours its waters will overrun his farm. This gives him a little foreknowledge of the coming flood, and he does what any good farmer would do. He immediately takes his cattle and everything else that he can move to higher ground where they will be saved from the dangerous waters. This he does on the basis of foreknowledge.

God, however, is not limited to 24-hour foreknowledge. He foresees all things in our lives and does something about them.

Predestination

The word "predestinate" indicates that God has set His heart on doing something for us. He has a goal in view and He is going to see that we reach the image of His Son. He knows what it will take to bring us into conformity to His Son and, therefore, sets out to do this.

The word "predestinate" can well be used in connection with the work of our Lord Jesus Christ. Long before the foundation of the world, God the Father, God the Son and God the Holy Spirit, uniting in one purpose for the welfare of man, determined that Jesus, the eternal Son, was to be the One Who would come at an appointed time and take upon Himself flesh and blood and die for the sins of man. Remember now, this was the determination of God long before the foundation of the world. God having all knowledge knew not only what things would happen but planned the happening, part of which was the determination that Jesus would die for us. God controlled all history in order to bring this to pass.

The same word is used in connection with God's purposes for the Christian. "Whom he [God] did foreknow, he also did predestinate to be conformed to the image of his Son." It is God's determined purpose that such will be the goal in the life of each one of us who has trusted in Christ. That is the basic reason for things that take place in our lives. Nothing can change God's purpose in this, no matter what the opposition may be. Satan has entered the scene and has attempted to thwart the purposes of God for each of us, but Satan cannot win. Jesus Christ through His death has already broken Satan's power. There is no time in our experience when we need to succumb to the enemy.

In dying, the Lord Jesus Christ died to sin, and we died with Him. For that reason the Adamic nature cannot overcome us and control us if we will submit ourselves to God and His love. God has vanquished all these foes for us through Christ in order that we might be conformed to the image of His Son.

There are many ways in which God will see this goal fulfilled in His children, one of which is described in Ephesians 4. First we are told of gifted men whom God has given as gifts to His people: "And he gave some, apostles; and some, prophets; and some, evangelists; and some, pastors and teachers" (v. 11). The next verse tells us why God has given us these men: "For the perfecting of the saints, for the work of the ministry, for the edifying of the body of Christ" (v. 12). This is the first part of the goal; the 13th verse indicates the ultimate end of it: "Till we all come in the unity of the faith, and of the knowledge of the Son of God, unto a perfect man, unto the measure of the stature of the fulness of Christ." The perfect man in this passage is the mature man, and the more mature we are in the Christian faith the more we are conformed to the image of God's Son. The same truth is expressed in the words, "unto the measure of the stature of the fulness of Christ."

The picture here is that of a body of which all of us are definite parts. There are different gifts presented all of which have different expressions of service; yet they all have one major purpose—to glorify the Lord Jesus. For each individual there is a detailed plan of life which is different from that for any other individual. God works with each of us and through each of us until we come to the unity of the faith and the knowledge of Christ, until we become mature in the fulness of Christ. Christ is set forth in this connection as an example for us. But more than that, God is so working that we are all moving together toward completion in Christ. He is the Head of the body, and we are that body. As the Head is perfect so the body will be conformed eventually to the Head. In this we see that God not only matures us individually, but collectively in the Body of Christ.

In verse 26 of this chapter we have the assurance that the Spirit of God is with us and for us. Then verses 28 through 31 assure us that God the Father is for us, and verse 34 tells us what Christ has done on our behalf. In verses 31 to 35, questions are raised with reference to those who may be against us, and in every case the answer reassures the believer of his complete protection through the salvation provided by the Lord Jesus Christ.

"In all these things we are more than conquerors through him that loved us. For I am persuaded, that neither death, nor life, nor angels, nor principalities, nor powers, nor things present, nor things to come, nor height, nor depth, nor any other creature, shall be able to separate us from the love of God, which is in Christ Jesus our Lord" (vv. 37-39).

This is what makes a "know-so" Christian instead of a "hope-so" Christian. Paul's persuasion was founded on truth. God's Word, he knew, was sure. It is no wonder he declared: "For I am persuaded, that neither death, nor life, nor angels, nor principalities, nor powers, nor things present, nor things to come, nor height, nor depth, nor any other creature, shall be able to separate us from the love of God, which is in Christ Jesus our Lord" (vv. 38,39). He realized there was nothing in this life—

not even death—regardless of how it might come, that could separate us from God.

In the light of such tremendous spiritual provision and such glorious triumph on the part of the believer, dare we hold back from God? Let us give ourselves over to Him completely so that the practical triumphs to be enjoyed in face of daily testings shall be witness to the world of the triumphant life in Christ.

Memory Assignment:
Memorize Romans 8:28.

EXAMINATION

Circle the correct letter:
1. When a person receives Christ as Saviour, the Holy Spirit
   a. removes his infirmities.
   b. helps his infirmities.
   c. is not concerned about his infirmities.
2. The weaknesses or infirmities spoken of in Romans 8:26 specifically have to do with our
   a. bodies.
   b. minds.
   c. prayer life.
3. The intercession of the Holy Spirit is made
   a. in us.
   b. in heaven.
   c. at the right hand of the Father.
4. "He that searcheth the hearts" (Rom. 8:27) refers to
   a. God the Father.
   b. God the Son.
   c. God the Holy Spirit.
5. A passage that should be considered with Romans 8:28 is
   a. James 4:6-8.
   b. Hebrews 4:12.
   c. Galatians 3:22-24.

Complete the following.

6. God never tempts us with _____.

7. Some trials seem to bring us no benefit, but it is when they work _____ that they become good for us.

8. God knows what is in the future because to His infinite knowledge all time is as if it were _____.

9. Among other things, God has predestinated the Christian to be conformed to the _____ of His _____.

10. We need not succumb to the enemy because in Christ's death He broke _____ power.

True or False:

11. _____ "Teachers" are listed among the gifted men which God has given to the Church.

12. _____ God's purpose in giving gifted men to the Church is that we might all come to the unity of the faith.

13. _____ The purpose of having many different gifts among God's people is to put attention on the individual believer.

14. _____ Romans 8:31-35 reassures the believer of his complete protection through the salvation provided by Christ.

15. _____ Only death separates a person from the love of God.

☐ I have memorized Romans 8:28.

unit 8

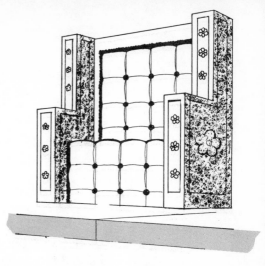

The Sovereignty of God

Contrary to what some excellent commentaries on Romans say, I do not consider chapters 9, 10 and 11 to be parenthetical. I believe they are an integral part of the book. Without them a vital aspect of truth would be missing.

Though man's basic need is that of salvation, there is just as great a need for the person who is saved to learn to live by faith the life provided by the indwelling Christ. This is the subject of Romans 6, 7 and 8. There is the danger of the Lord not being pleased with us even as He was not with the Israelites when they failed to walk a life of faith (I Cor. 10:4,5). We need to study what happened to Israel, for "these things happened unto them for ensamples: and they are written for our admonition" (I Cor. 10:11).

The great love in Paul's heart for Israel is clearly disclosed in the opening verses of Romans 9. Paul would have been willing to have been accursed himself if it would have meant that his fellow Jews might be saved.

After declaring his great love for Israel, Paul enumerates several advantages which the nation Israel had over other nations. These are given in two verses: "Who are Israelites; to whom pertaineth the adoption, and the glory, and the covenants, and the giving of the law, and the service of God, and the promises; Whose are the fathers, and of whom as concerning the flesh Christ came, who is over all, God blessed for ever. Amen" (vv. 4,5).

The Adoption

First of all, to Israel pertained the adoption. Israel was placed as a particular nation in a particular place to fulfill a particular purpose. This is the testimony of Deuteronomy 14:2: "For thou art an holy people unto the Lord thy God, and the Lord hath chosen thee to be a peculiar people unto himself, above all the nations that are upon the earth."

The Glory

The second special advantage to Israel was the Shekinah glory. God manifested Himself in a unique way to Israel. The pillar of cloud by day and the pillar of fire by night led them wherever they needed to go. These were visible demonstrations of the presence of God in their midst and showed the Israelites when they were to move and when they were to remain. The glory of the Shekinah also filled the tabernacle at certain times.

The Covenants

The third great benefit of Israel is the covenants God made with her. There were several of these. The one which was basic to all the others was the Abrahamic Covenant. This promised a national land to Israel (Gen. 12:1; 13:14,15,17); a redemption which would have both national and universal significance (Gen. 12:3; 22:18; Gal. 3:16); and the promise of a large number of descendents who would make a great nation (Gen. 12:2; 13:16; 17:2-6).

The Palestinian Covenant is concerned with the conditions under which Israel entered into the land of promise (Deut. 30:1-10). It forms Israel's title deed to the land, a title deed written by God.

The Davidic Covenant is concerned with the establishment of a worldwide kingdom under Christ, David's greater son (II Sam. 7:12-17). The nation has failed to meet some of its responsibilities and as a consequence has been temporarily laid aside. Nevertheless, through them Jesus Christ, the Messiah, did come, and He will one day sit upon the Throne of David and rule the entire world.

God has also promised to make a New Covenant with Israel. This is in contrast to the Mosaic Covenant which we will consider under the subject of the Law. The New Covenant is a future one and is outlined in Jeremiah 31:31-34. It promises to put God's law within the hearts of His people.

Israel was also chosen to receive the Law, sometimes called the Mosaic Covenant (Ex. 20:1-31:18). The Law system had to do with God's standards of righteousness. The individual laws were given to govern Israel's life on a national basis and on an individual basis.

The Law was given to Israel, not to the Gentiles. The purpose and time limit of the Law are revealed in Galatians 3:19: "It was added because of transgressions, till the seed should come to whom the promise was made."

The Service of God

To Israel also belonged the service of God. This refers to the sacrificial and ceremonial system of the tabernacle and the temple. No other nation had such a privilege of entering into the very presence of God—into the Holy of Holies through the blood shed on the day of atonement. All of the great ceremonies and sacrifices of the tabernacle and temple pointed forward to Christ. He was the substance of which they were the shadow (Col. 2:16,17).

The Promises

The phrase "the promises" emphasizes that aspect of the promises made to Abraham concerning Christ. He brings peace and righteousness to the individual heart and will bring the same to the earth when He comes again. God's promise to Abraham was that peace should come to the world from One who would be a descendent of Abraham so far as the flesh is concerned.

The Fathers

The "Fathers" were the men who laid the great national foundations for Israel. Abraham, Isaac and Jacob were the physical roots out of which God brought the nation. The ancestry of each Israelite goes back some 4000 years to Abraham.

Christ

The final benefit mentioned in Romans 9 which Israel had over the other nations is found in the words: "Of whom as concerning the flesh Christ came." Israel was the physical channel through which the Lord of glory came in the flesh. This is brought before us in the very first chapter of Romans where we read: "Concerning his Son Jesus Christ our Lord, which was made of the seed of David according to the flesh" (v. 3).

The Sovereignty of God

Why did God set Israel aside even temporarily? Did He have a right to do so? Romans chapter 9 presents the truth of God's sovereignty—that He has the absolute right to choose and do as He desires.

After showing that not all physical Israel was spiritual Israel (v. 6), the Apostle Paul points out where God exercised His sovereignty in working out His affairs among men. It was in Isaac that Abraham's seed was to be called—not in Ishmael. This was a sovereign choice made by God; nothing that Abraham could do would set it aside.

God's dealing with Jacob and Esau is another illustration of His sovereign choice with regard to men and their part in His plans (9:10-13). In choosing Jacob, God was not choosing him for salvation. That is not the subject in these verses. The possibility of being saved was as free to Esau as it was to Jacob. By looking back at the character of these two men we realize that God knew what He was doing when He chose Jacob instead of Esau. The choice was not for salvation but for having a place in the line from which Christ should come according to the flesh.

The word "hated" in verse 13 is not hate as we normally think of it. Rather, it is a matter of preferring one thing over another.

Sovereign Mercy

God declared to Moses: "I will have mercy on whom I will have mercy, and I will have compassion on whom I will have compassion" (9:15). God did not say He would send to hell those He wanted sent there. He never uses His electing grace to send anyone to hell. The Apostle Paul asks, "Is there unrighteousness with God?" and then answers with a strong negative: "God forbid" (v. 14). We have no right to summon God to the bar of justice and say He is wrong. He has chosen to have mercy on all who will accept His mercy.

God is the Divine Potter (vv. 20,21). Israel could not justly complain against God's judgments for except for His mercy they would have been wiped out at the beginning of their desert journey to Canaan.

A second illustration of God's sovereign choice of mercy is seen in the life of Pharaoh (vv. 17,18). Because of the phrase, "Therefore hath he mercy on whom he will have mercy, and whom he will he hardeneth," many have asked, "How can God deliberately harden a man's heart, and then condemn him for what he does?" We must remember that the Lord did not harden Pharaoh's heart to begin with. Pharaoh hardened his own heart, a fact which is clearly stated in I Samuel 6:6: "Wherefore then do ye harden your hearts, as the Egyptians and Pharaoh hardened their hearts? when he had wrought wonderfully among them, did they not let the people go, and they departed?"

God knew beforehand what Pharaoh would do and how he would treat Israel and reject God's purposes for His people. God saw Pharaoh as a man who would always reject Him; yet God in His foreknowledge did not decree that this was the kind of man Pharaoh must be. God has chosen to act in mercy, and when He acts in judgment it is because men have refused to accept His mercy.

God does not in any case elect or predestinate any human being to destruction or wrath or death. At the Great White Throne Judgment the destiny of those appearing there is the second death. Yet this will be the consequence of their own rejection of the only means of spiritual life. They will face wrath because they themselves have rejected mercy. To refuse the way of life is to accept the way of death.

Israel lost out because they did not accept God's grace and salvation. The whole law pointed to Christ and to the fact that man could become righteous simply by believing. Man is not able to fulfill the requirements of the Law. The Israelites stumbled over Christ, never seeing the real purpose of the Law which was to bring them to Christ. This was why God rejected them. It was because of their unbelief. It was for this reason that He temporarily set them aside as a nation.

True righteousness before God is gained only by faith in Christ. This is why Paul says in verse 30: "What shall we say then? That the Gentiles, which followed not after righteousness, have attained to righteousness, even the righteousness which is of faith." Here was a people who were not chosen of God as was Israel. The Gentiles were a people outside of God's special dealings, but they found righteousness because they received it by faith. It was this righteousness of God which is manifested "by the law and the prophets; Even the righteousness of God which is by faith of Jesus Christ unto all and upon all them that believe: for there is no difference" (3:21,22).

Israel followed after the law of righteousness but did not attain to it because they sought it by the works of the Law instead of by faith. When Christ came, Israel rejected Him. They were persuaded that their own self-righteousness was sufficient to take care of their obligations before God.

The question of how Israel who was so favored could be rejected and the Gentiles not favored could be accepted is the question raised and answered at the end of chapter 9. The answer is, as we have seen, that the Gentiles received the gift of righteousness by faith which Israel refused to do. The Law considers us all under sin in order that God might have mercy upon all. There is no difference in the Jew or the Gentile in this respect because all have sinned and come short of the glory of God.

The crucial question is not, What does the Law think of me? but, What do I think of Christ? It is no longer a matter of our righteousness but His righteousness. It is no longer our works, but His finished work. It is not so much the sin question as it is the Son question. When we receive the Son into our lives, the sin question is taken care of.

Christ is still the stumblingblock to many today. The intellectual worships his wisdom. The rich man trusts in his wealth. The moralist leans on his personal excellence. To all of these Christ is a stumblingblock.

Memory Assignment:
Memorize Romans 9:4,5.

EXAMINATION

True or False:

1. ____ Romans 9, 10 and 11 are parenthetical chapters in the Book of Romans.
2. ____ Paul would have been willing to be accursed if it would have meant that his fellow Jews might be saved.
3. ____ In Romans 9:4,5 Paul lists several advantages which the Jews had over the Gentile nations.
4. ____ The "glory" that Israel had is a reference to her proud patriotism.
5. ____ The record of the Palestinian Covenant is found in Deuteronomy 30.

Complete the following.

6. The Old Testament Law is sometimes called the _____ Covenant.

7. The ancestry of each Jew goes back some 4000 years to _____.

8. Romans 9 presents the truth of God's _____.

9. The choice between Jacob and Esau was not for salvation but for determining who would be in the _____ of _____.

10. Regardless of whether we understand God's work of choosing or not, we still must agree with Paul that there is no _____ with God (Rom. 9:14).

Circle the correct letter:

11. In Romans 9:20,21 God is compared to a
    a. father.
    b. baker.
    c. potter.

12. God acts in judgment on
    a. whomever He chooses.
    b. those who reject His mercy.
    c. no one, for He is a God of love.
13. The Israelites stumbled over Christ because they never saw the
    a. real purpose of the Law.
    b. promises in the Scriptures.
    c. the power of God displayed.
14. Israel did not attain unto the law of righteousness because
    a. God did not want them to.
    b. they sought it by the works of the Law.
    c. they did not know they needed salvation.
15. The Gentiles received the gift of righteousness because
    a. they deserved it more than Israel.
    b. they accepted it by faith.
    c. they had more good works than Israel.

☐ I have memorized Romans 9:4,5.

unit 9

God's Righteousness Versus Self-Righteousness

"Brethren, my heart's desire and prayer to God for Israel is, that they might be saved. For I bear them record that they have a zeal of God, but not according to knowledge. For they being ignorant of God's righteousness, and going about to establish their own righteousness, have not submitted themselves unto the righteousness of God. For Christ is the end of the law for righteousness to every one that believeth. For Moses describeth the righteousness which is of the law, That the man which doeth those things shall live by them" (Rom. 10:1-5).

What we have called "self-righteousness" God speaks of as "their own righteousness." Israel's righteousness was a futile effort on their part to produce under and through the Law a character that they thought would please God. This is the same in principle that men attempt today when they try to be saved by their own works. The attitude of such is, "Well, I'm not so bad," or "I am living up to the Ten Commandments," or "I am living by the Golden Rule," or "I am doing the very best I can."

To produce a God-approved character by such means as these is utterly impossible. God has already declared that "by the deeds of the law, there shall no flesh be justified in his sight" and that "all have sinned and come short of the glory of God." This leaves us without the help of the Law. But God brings us to Christ for help that the Law could not give when He says,

"Christ is the end of the law for righteousness to every one that believeth."

Over against self-righteousness we have God's righteousness. Israel of old did not submit "themselves unto the righteousness of God." This is not speaking here of an attribute of God nor is it the changed character of the believer. It is not something that God is, nor a change that He works in us so that we do everything that pleases Him. The expression "the righteousness of God" is Christ himself. He met the demand of the perfect Law, proving before God and man that He kept every point of the Law. Then He died in our place. He is made unto us righteousness according to I Corinthians 1:30. This is what Paul meant in Romans 3:22 when he said, "Even the righteousness of God which is by faith of Jesus Christ unto all and upon all them that believe."

This righteousness which our Lord accomplished was put to our account. It was imputed to us when we believed on Christ. Through faith in Christ we are given a right standing before God.

The moment we trust Christ as Saviour righteousness is imputed to us, that is, it is put to our account. At the same time, God begins a work in us whereby His righteousness is imparted to us, and this is a continuing work throughout our experience on earth. It is Christ in us, the living Christ, working out His life through us. This is the second aspect of the Christian life.

Israel had a zeal for God, "but not according to knowledge," said Paul. Religious zeal is commendable but it can be very much in error and miss God's plan altogether. A person can be as sincere as he pleases but God looks for more than mere sincerity. It is possible to be sincere and yet be totally mistaken. Our sincerity in trying to work for salvation does not alter the fact that we are lost. We can be as sincere as we please, but it does not mean that we are saved.

Christ, we are told, "is the end of the law for righteousness for every one that believeth." For us to try to keep the Law in order to establish our own right standing with God is nothing short of rejecting Christ. The Law was consummated in Christ. He fulfilled it completely.

Even though Christ has become the end of the Law for righteousness this does not mean that we have been set free from the Law so that we can steal, lie, murder, or break the Law in anyway we please. There is a new law, the law of Christ which is His life in us that causes us to desire the things of God, and the Holy Spirit empowers us to live the Christ-life so as to please God. The Mosaic Law said, "Do and ye shall live." The law of Christ says, "Live and ye shall do." According to I Corinthians 9:21 we are not "without law to God, but under the law to Christ."

Way of Salvation

Verses 9 and 10 of Romans 10 make perfectly clear what is required for the experience of salvation: "That if thou shalt confess with thy mouth the Lord Jesus, and shalt believe in thine heart that God hath raised him from the dead, thou shalt be saved. For with the heart man believeth unto righteousness; and with the mouth confession is made unto salvation."

It is with confession that we identify ourselves with Christ, and the confession involved is that Jesus is the Lord. With the heart faith is expressed. To confess with the mouth and leave the heart out of the transaction would be hypocrisy. To have a heart faith without a mouth confession would be cowardice.

"The scripture saith, Whosoever believeth on him shall not be ashamed. For there is no difference between the Jew and the Greek: for the same Lord over all is rich unto all that call upon him. For whosoever shall call upon the name of the Lord shall be saved" (vv. 11-13). All men have the same need, and the same means of salvation is provided for all. All men are born in the same way—by natural birth. All men can only be born again in the same way—through faith in Christ.

Salvation is an individual and personal matter. The Jew is not saved because he is a Jew. Neither can we be saved because we belong to the right church. Here we have the way of salvation plainly set before us: "Whosoever shall call upon the name of the Lord shall be saved." The Scripture does not say that all will be saved, but that those who call on the Lord shall be saved.

Salvation rests in one man, the man Christ Jesus. God has not given us a set of rules or regulations or creeds or dogmas that we are to meticulously follow and thus be saved. Rather, He has given us a man, a person, His own Son who is the truth and the life and the way. He does not merely represent the truth and show the way, but He is the Truth and the Life and the Way. Salvation is in the person of the Lord Jesus Christ.

In this passage we are next brought to our responsibilities as believers to proclaim the gospel: "How then shall they call on him in whom they have not believed? and how shall they believe in him of whom they have not heard? and how shall they hear without a preacher? And how shall they preach, except they be sent?" (vv. 14,15).

God had set the nation of Israel as a light to reveal to the nations of the world the one true God. They were to be God's representatives to tell the world of the Saviour. Israel utterly failed at this point. Then the message was taken to the Gentiles and the Gentiles are failing just as Israel did.

To us has been committed the message of reconciliation and we are to so live that others may know the hope of our calling and desire to have the relationship with Christ which we have.

Four Questions

There are four questions in verses 14 and 15 which apply first of all to Israel. But the same truth has its application in our lives.

The first question is: "How then shall they call on him in whom they have not believed?" The words "call" and "believe" are connected. "Calling" suggests action; "believing" on the other hand is somewhat passive. "Believing" is an act of the mind whereas "calling" is an act of the will. "Believing" is more what we think about something. "Calling" is what we do about it. It is not enough to say that we believe. It is only enough when we act upon our faith. Faith is no mere acquiescence to some fact but acting upon that fact.

The second question is: "How shall they believe in him of whom they have not heard?" In this passage hearing is linked with a person. The believing is to be a believing in Christ. How can persons believe in Christ if they have not heard of Him? This means there must be a definite tangible someone to believe in. This is no abstraction, no religious feeling, but definite faith in a definite person designated by God.

The third question is: "How shall they hear without a preacher?" This speaks of human agency. Calling requires believing, and believing requires hearing, and hearing requires telling.

The gospel is not self-discovered. It is not something we dig out for ourselves. It is something we receive only from God.

God uses personalities to transmit His message. He has committed this message to men but not to angels. Men who can demonstrate what it is to believe are also to proclaim what they believe. This is the message of Romans 6, 7 and 8. Consequently, hearing includes not only the hearing with the ear but also learning through the eyegate. Speaking, radio, literature—whichever way God wants the message given out—we should see that it is proclaimed. The early church had its responsibility to some 250 million people. Today we have the responsibility of reaching 3 billion people. But God's provision for this day is ample if we consider radio and literature. Nevertheless, it is still a matter of person to person so far as the gospel is concerned.

The fourth question is: "And how shall they preach except they be sent?" The commission is plain. There is first of all divine authority to proclaim. Then there is human assistance. God has said, "Let him that is taught in the word communicate unto him [share with him] that teacheth." If we are not called to preach, we are called to let others go and lend them the necessary assistance to go with the message.

There is a chain reaction in all of this. The sending results in telling, the telling in hearing, the hearing in believing, the believing in calling, and the calling in God's answer with salvation. Where do we fit into this picture? None can escape the commission, and none can escape the loss of reward when the commission is not met.

It is important then to recognize that faith can only come by hearing. And we Christians are laborers together with God and with each other in this commission that is worldwide in its responsibility.

Memory Assignment:
Memorize Romans 10:9,10.

EXAMINATION

True or False:
1. _____ What we speak of as Israel's "self-righteousness" God speaks of as "their own righteousness."
2. _____ It is possible to be justified by the deeds of the Law.
3. _____ The phrase, "The righteousness of God," refers to Christ Himself.
4. _____ Christ's righteousness is imputed to the Christian when he reaches spiritual maturity.
5. _____ For us to try to keep the Law in order to establish our righteousness is the same as rejecting Christ.

Complete the following.
6. In the place of the Mosaic Law, the Christian is under a new law called the law of _____.
7. To confess with the mouth without a heart experience, is _____.
8. "For _____ shall _____ upon the name of the _____ shall be _____" (Rom. 10:13).
9. Instead of a set of rules on how to be saved, God has given us a _____.
10. Romans 10:14,15 presents our _____ as believers to proclaim the _____.

Circle the correct letter:
11. To the Christian has been committed the message of
   a. judgment.
   b. the Kingdom.
   c. reconciliation.
12. The word "call" is connected in its meaning with
   a. repenting.
   b. believing.
   c. exhorting.

13. The word "believe" in Romans 10:14 has to do with believing
    a. that there is a God.
    b. that all will be saved.
    c. in Christ as the way of salvation.
14. God's provision for reaching the present age is ample if we consider
    a. we have less people to reach today than the early church per capita.
    b. we have radio, literature and other mass means of spreading the gospel.
    c. that people are turning to Christ today with less effort on our part.
15. Before a person can place faith in Christ he must first
    a. hear about Christ.
    b. turn from his old life.
    c. be baptized.

☐   I have memorized Romans 10:9,10.

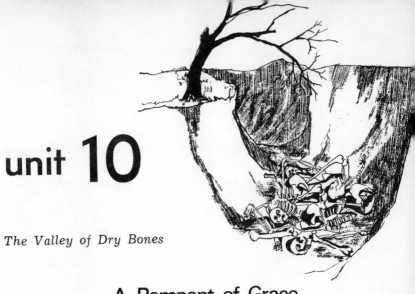

unit 10

The Valley of Dry Bones

A Remnant of Grace

The Apostle Paul begins chapter 11 of Romans with a question and some very clear answers to it: "I say then, Hath God cast away his people? God forbid. For I also am an Israelite, of the seed of Abraham, of the tribe of Benjamin. God hath not cast away his people which he foreknew" (vv. 1,2).

Paul assures us in this portion of Scripture that God has not cast off His people forever. The fact that there are individual Israelites saved during the present age proves God has not cast off His people permanently. Paul himself was a living example.

Romans 11:6 sets forth a very important principle: "And if by grace, then is it no more of works: otherwise grace is no more grace. But if it be of works, then is it no more grace: otherwise work is no more work." Once works is added to grace, grace is no longer grace. Individual salvation is all of grace and not of works. The same will be true in the bringing back of the people of Israel. Grace must be accepted and appropriated for salvation by the individual, and so must it be for Israel's national salvation.

Israel will yet be brought back to God and gathered once more to her homeland. She will experience national restoration and national blessing. Today, the nation of Israel is small in number, but we see a new development in that after 2000 years there is an independent state of Israel in Palestine. Although most of the Jews in the world are still scattered among the

Gentile nations, there are some returning to their ancient homeland. They are doing this, however, in spiritual unbelief.

Israel's Blindness

Romans 11:25 tells us that "blindness in part" has happened
to Israel. This spiritual blindness, however, is not something
that has settled on the minds and hearts of every Israelite, for
there are some who are turning to Christ and being saved today.
But for the most part, the nation is still in darkness with regard
to Christ.

There is a time element involved with regard to this partial
blindness. It will not last forever. A great change will come
and so many Jews will receive the Saviour that the Scriptures
say, "All Israel shall be saved" (11:26). In this same verse there
is a play on words. In one phrase the word "Israel" is used and
in the last phrase the word "Jacob" is used. What is the difference between "Israel" and "Jacob" as used in such prophetic
Scriptures? For the most part, the word "Jacob" refers to the
natural posterity of Israel—it refers to those who have physical
descent but not necessarily spiritual life. The word "Israel"
stresses spiritual relationship with God.

Zechariah 13:8,9 indicates that two-thirds of the nation of
Israel will be destroyed during the Tribulation, but that the one-
third that is left will be brought through the time of Jacob's
trouble and gloriously saved. It is clear both from the Old and
New Testaments that God has not cast off His people either
totally or finally. Individual salvation is possible for any Israelite
who wants to accept Christ and be saved now. God has not cast
away the nation finally because it is a nation that at a future
time will be born in a day and go on to serve Christ in His
millennial kingdom. From this nation in the past has come our
Bible and our Christ. In the future when Christ rules over it,
world peace and world prosperity will also come from this nation
to the world.

When Christ rules as sovereign Lord from the city of Jerusalem during the Millennium, famine, slavery and savagery will
be things of the past and everlasting peace will be established.
But world peace will never be achieved by man's efforts as such
peace will not exist until Christ personally returns to earth to
establish His rule.

Before this takes place, blood will flow in Palestine and the surrounding areas such as it has never done before. The armies of the earth will be united in their hatred for Jesus Christ, but He will destroy them in the world's greatest battle.

Why did God permit blindness and hardness in Israel? The answer is found in Romans 11:11: "Have they stumbled that they should fall? God forbid: but rather through their fall salvation is come unto the Gentiles, for to provoke them to jealousy." This was not a fall that would eventually destroy them. But they were made blind so that the gospel could come to the Gentiles. Even those among the Jews who accepted the Lord as Saviour had difficulty in accepting Gentiles into the family of God. Paul and Peter both experienced this prejudice as they sought to preach the gospel.

A second reason that blindness is happened to Israel is that the Gentiles might become proof of God's true plan and purpose in Christ Jesus and thus provoke Israel to jealousy. The Jews were a people who had tried to attain to righteousness in their own way and not God's way. So God said He would take a people that was not His people and reveal through them His plans and purposes. Christ would dwell in each believer's heart and on the basis of faith demonstrate His life in them.

This was not a foreign truth to Israel. God had presented it to them right along. Abraham believed God and it was accounted to him for righteousness. It was not because of the works he did but because he believed God that he was reckoned righteous.

A Gentile Warning

A warning, however, is given to the Gentiles in Romans 11:25: "For I would not, brethren, that ye should be ignorant of this mystery, lest ye should be wise in your own conceits; that blindness in part is happened to Israel, until the fulness of the Gentiles be come in." Israel's blindness is only until God completes His work among the Gentiles. All during this time individuals are offered salvation according to the election of grace.

We must distinguish clearly between the "times of the Gentiles" and the "fulness of the Gentiles." The "fulness of the Gentiles" has to do with the completing of the Body of Christ. The "times of the Gentiles" has to do with the period of time that Jerusalem will be under the control of Gentile nations. When the times of the Gentiles are fulfilled, that is, when the Gentiles' cup of iniquity is full, then God will restore Israel to her wonderful place in His program. His judgment will fall upon the Gentile nations for their awful sins, many of which are piling up before our very eyes today.

God is seeking to provoke Israel to jealousy through His work in the lives of us who belong to the Body of Christ. Paul wrote in verses 13,14: "For I speak to you Gentiles, inasmuch as I am the apostle of the Gentiles, I magnify mine office: If by any means I may provoke to emulation them which are my flesh, and might save some of them." Paul wanted to provoke his natural kin, the people of Israel, to jealousy. It is when they see us living victoriously the life of the indwelling Christ that they will desire what Christ has to offer. But can they see this? Are they seeing in us what the Law could not produce in them and what it cannot produce in us?

Valley of Dry Bones

Israel's temporary blindness and her final regathering are subjects covered in chapter 37 of Ezekiel. The vivid picture presented there is that of a valley of dry bones. As the Prophet Ezekiel stood among them God asked him: "Can these bones live?" Ezekiel then prophesied as he was commanded and said, "There was a noise, and behold a shaking, and the bones came together, bone to his bone. And when I beheld, lo, the sinews and the flesh came up upon them, and the skin covered them above: but there was no breath in them" (vv. 7,8).

For some 2000 years Israel has been as dry bones. Nationally they have been dormant, but that condition will not last indefinitely. We have witnessed a partial regathering of Israel in our day. But it is not a regathering because of spiritual life. Just as these bones came together and were covered by skin but no life was present, so is Israel's spiritual condition today. They are gathered together in unbelief.

But God did not stop with this. Ezekiel was instructed to prophesy to the wind, and to breathe upon the slain that they might live. Ezekiel said he prophesied "as he [God] commanded me, and the breath came into them, and they lived, and stood up upon their feet, an exceeding great army."

This is what will happen to Israel when they see the Lord Jesus Christ coming in glory. They will see Him stand upon the

Mount of Olives and will look on Him whom they have pierced, and will suddenly turn to Him in faith.

It is with this background that we can now turn to verses 16-18 of Romans 11: "For if the firstfruit be holy, the lump is also holy: and if the root be holy, so are the branches. And if some of the branches be broken off, and thou, being a wild olive tree, wert graffed in among them, and with them partakest of the root and fatness of the olive tree; Boast not against the branches. But if thou boast, thou bearest not the root, but the root thee."

This is God's way of picturing how the Gentiles have been graffed into the root, which represents Israel, the natural olive tree. If some of the branches have been broken off so that we, being a wild olive tree, might be graffed in among them, then we partake "of the root and fatness of the olive tree." Then we are warned, "Boast not against the branches. But if thou boast, thou bearest not the root, but the root thee" (v. 18). There is nothing for us to boast in. The great spiritual blessings—the Bible, the Lord Jesus Christ—came by way of Israel. We are also told, "Salvation is of the Jews." We benefit by the gospel because of God's wonderful grace through Israel. So we are warned not to become haughty and proud. The branches that were broken off because of unbelief were Israel. We stand by faith, so there is no room for being high-minded but every reason for a reverential fear: "For if God spared not the natural branches, take heed lest he also spare not thee."

The severity of God toward Israel because of their unbelief is unmistakably clear in the Scriptures and in history. Their city and temple were destroyed. Their land was made desolate. They were killed by the thousands and the remainder were scattered throughout the Gentile nations. This final severe judgment took place in A.D. 70, and Israel's sorrows are not yet over.

There are signs connected with God's future program for Israel: "And there shall be signs in the sun, and in the moon, and in the stars; and upon the earth distress of nations, with perplexity; the sea and the waves roaring; Men's hearts failing them for fear, and for looking after those things which are coming on the earth: for the powers of heaven shall be shaken. And then shall they see the Son of man coming in a cloud with power and great glory. And when these things begin to come to pass, then look up, and lift up your heads; for your redemption draweth nigh" (Luke 21:25-28).

The time of Israel's blindness will last during the gathering in of the Church which is the Body of Christ. After the Church is raptured from the earth God will again work with the nation Israel. At the end of the seven years of Tribulation Christ shall return to earth to judge the nations and establish His 1000-year rule from Jerusalem.

When Christ returns to earth at the end of the Tribulation the nation Israel will receive Him as their Redeemer and Sovereign King. In His first coming He came to die on a cross, but in His second coming He will come to sit upon a Throne. In His first coming He was shamefully treated, but in His second coming He will appear in glory and remove all ungodliness from His people.

It was after considering these things that the Apostle Paul broke forth with a benediction of highest praise: "O the depth of the riches both of the wisdom and knowledge of God! how unsearchable are his judgments, and his ways past finding out! For who hath known the mind of the Lord? or who hath been his counsellor? Or who hath first given to him, and it shall be recompensed unto him again? For of him, and through him, and to him, are all things: to whom be glory for ever. Amen" (11:33-36).

Memory Assignment:
Memorize Romans 11:25.

EXAMINATION

Circle the correct letter:

1. According to Romans 11:6, if something is of grace
   a. it cannot also be of works.
   b. it can also be of works.
   c. it has been earned.
2. For the most part, the Jewish people now going back to Palestine are doing so
   a. because they expect the Messiah.
   b. because they want to fulfill the Scriptures.
   c. in spiritual unbelief.
3. According to Zechariah 13:8,9, what part of the nation of Israel will be destroyed in the Tribulation?
   a. One-third.
   b. One-half.
   c. Two-thirds.
4. World peace will be attained by
   a. governments during the present age.
   b. Christ during the Millennium.
   c. no person or group in the realm of this world.
5. In the world's greatest battle, the victor will be
   a. Russia.
   b. the United States.
   c. Christ.

Complete the following.

6. The blindness of Israel turned out to the benefit of the

   _____.

7. Abraham was saved because he _____ God.

8. "Blindness in part is happened to Israel, until the _____ of the _____ be come in" (Rom. 11:25).

9. When the Gentiles' cup of iniquity is full, then God will _____ Israel to her place in His program.

10. Through His work in our lives, God is seeking to provoke Israel to _____.

True or False:

11. _____ Israel will not turn to the Lord even when they see Him stand on the Mount of Olives at His second coming.

12. _____ Israel is as a branch which has been broken off and replaced by another and, therefore, will never be restored as a branch again.

13. _____ As a nation, Israel was plundered and scattered in A.D. 70.

14. _____ After the Church, which is the Body of Christ, has been raptured from the earth, God will again work with Israel.

15. _____ Christ will establish His 1000-year reign in peace on the earth after the 7 years of Tribulation are past.

☐   I have memorized Romans 11:25.

unit 11

The Appeal

To keep the information gathered from our studies in Romans as mere head knowledge will cause us to go backward in the Christian life rather than to advance. We must make a definite decision on the basis of these great truths. This is an established principle of God's working as the Word very clearly points out.

Exactly the same principle was employed by Paul when he said, "I beseech you therefore, brethren, by the mercies of God, that ye present your bodies a living sacrifice" (Rom. 12:1). The phrase "mercies of God," refers to the preceding chapters in Romans and the truths presented in them. It is on the basis of what God has done for us that this appeal for the presenting of our bodies is made.

The question before us now is, What are we going to do about it? Surely there can be only one answer and that is the one Paul gave when he said, "The love of Christ constraineth us." Can we, in the face of such love, compassion, such abundant provision, protection, security, and assurance in Christ Jesus say to God, "We will wait until we get to heaven to enjoy these things." Will we not rather do something about it now?

This love constrains us to do the very things that God wants us to do. Having the Spirit of adoption within us whereby we cry, "Abba, Father," let us go on to place ourselves completely in His hands.

We turn again to Paul's words, "I beseech you therefore, brethren, by the mercies of God." This appeal is based on the past mercies God has shown us. The word translated "by" in this passage has several meanings. The passage could be rendered "because of the mercies of God," and this is our first thought as we use the word "by" in this connection. But it can also mean "through" the mercy of God, the mercy He now extends to us. Because Christ died for our sins, God does not hold us who have trusted in Christ responsible for these sins any longer, so it is through the mercies of God that we are enjoined to present our bodies.

Yielding Our Bodies

From our study in Romans chapter 6, we learn that the word "present" is the same as the word "yield" where we read, "Neither yield ye your members as instruments of unrighteousness unto sin: but yield yourselves unto God, as those that are alive from the dead, and your members as instruments of righteousness unto God." The idea is that we are to present, or turn over, or put our bodies at God's disposal.

But why the body? The reason is that the body is the vehicle through which we operate. We must not confuse the old nature with the body. The old nature is part of the old, unregenerate life which seeks to control the body in order to practice evil. Think rather of the body as being a neutral vehicle in which we are living. By neutral we mean that it is neither good nor bad in itself. Before we were saved, the flesh nature controlled the body. Now that we have been born again, we are united to Christ so that the new man, the new nature, should be in control of the body. The Lord Jesus says, "I need the body, for that is the vehicle through which I show forth My life. I want the body as a living sacrifice." Now a living sacrifice is a paradox. Sacrifice is death, yet here He speaks of a living sacrifice. The fact is He wants both in our body—life and death. How can this be realized?

In the Old Testament sacrifices, animals were brought as offering for sin. But in their case it was death that God asked for, so that sacrifice and death go together. But in our case He asks for a living sacrifice. He wants our bodies while we are alive on this earth, but He wants us to live in the attitude of being dead to sin but alive to God. This is the basis for New Testament Christian living. Consequently, the words "living sacrifice" instead of being a paradox are now seen to be the recipe for the whole Christian life. We are to carry an attitude of death toward the old sinful nature and sinful things, and reckon ourselves alive toward God. For this reason, then, He wants our bodies to be given over entirely to Him.

Our eyes, which were once used to look at things that our bodies craved, are now to be given over to Him as separated holy members, to see the things He wants us to see. That in effect is already a sacrifice, a living sacrifice and a holy sacrifice.

Our ears, which were once given to listening to gossip, and our mouths which were once given to spreading that gossip, telling lies about people, murdering character, are now to be given over to Him to hear the cry of the spiritually poor and needy, and to tell them of life in Christ. Nothing short of that is acceptable with God.

Acceptable Service to God

We are not only told to present our bodies as living sacrifices unto God, but we are also told that when we yield them for this purpose they are holy and acceptable unto God. Such is worth careful study. Too many times we consider only what is acceptable to men. Our first consideration is often, "What will men think of what I am doing?" rather than "What does God think of it?" If we are singing, our first consideration may be the acceptability of our talent before men. We wonder if we will receive congratulations for what we have done. But it is far more important that we ask, "Is this thing acceptable to God?"

We are reminded again of Israel's experience as related in the Book of Malachi. God accused them of offering Him polluted bread on His altar, and they had the audacity to say, "Wherein have we polluted thee?" His answer was, "In that ye say, the table of the Lord is contemptible" (Mal. 1:7).

God continues the indictment in these words: "And if ye offer the blind for sacrifice, is it not evil? and if ye offer the lame and the sick, is it not evil? offer it now unto thy governor; will he be pleased with thee, or accept thy person? saith the Lord of hosts" (v. 8).

The Lord demanded that only the best was to be brought for sacrifice, but the Israelites brought the sick and the lame, animals for which there was little use. These they would not miss very much. But God reminded them that if they brought such gifts to their earthly rulers, they would not get by with it.

The message for us is obvious. Our various governments, local and federal, come along and tell us what percentage of our income and property is taxable and how much they want from us, and that is what they get. Yet so often in our finances we treat God as the Israelites treated Him with their offerings. Actually, all we have belongs to God, and yet He allows us to keep the largest portion of it for our own use.

The New Testament standard of giving is proportionate giving as outlined in I Corinthians 16, but so many of us give, not according to what we receive, but what we have left over after we have met our other obligations. Some will say, "I have so many debts and I do not think I should rob my creditors in order to pay God." But when we fail to give God His share, who are we actually robbing?

The answer again is found in Malachi: "But ye have profaned it, in that ye say, The table of the Lord is polluted; and the fruit thereof, even his meat, is contemptible. Ye said also, Behold, what a weariness is it! and ye have snuffed at it, saith the Lord of hosts; and ye brought . . . an offering: should I accept this of your hand? saith the Lord. But cursed be the deceiver, which hath in his flock a male, and voweth, and sacrificeth unto the Lord a corrupt thing: for I am a great King, saith the Lord of hosts, and my name is dreadful among the heathen" (vv. 12-14). The lesson to us is clear. Let us yield our bodies to God, for that is acceptable to Him. Let us give Him our strength and the best of our time. He deserves the best we have.

This He says is reasonable service. He has given all; can we give less? In the light of all that God has done for us in Christ, the least we can do is to give ourselves completely over to Him. He wants us exclusively for Himself.

Why is it that God's work seems, in many places at least, to go begging? Is it God's fault? He first gave us His Son and He will not withhold any lesser gift for our benefit. The problem and the responsibility are ours.

The Christian and the World

The next phrase introduces an attitude God wants us to hold to the world. It reads, "And be not conformed to this world." A better translation might be, "Be not fashioned after or pressed into the mold of this age." This brings before us the subject of worldliness for which many people have a ready definition. They identify worldliness as this kind of action or that kind of action, or by the way people dress.

We cannot measure worldliness in this way. Worldliness is an attitude of mind toward the things of this age. It is true, of course, that fashions can be such that a Christian cannot go along with them. It is a shame how, in these modern days, people are showing off so much of their bodies, often in such a way as to emphasize sex appeal which the world is playing up these days. But we must remember in all of this that worldliness goes deeper than mere outward appearance. It is a matter of the mind and the heart.

Rather than being conformed to this world, each Christian is admonished to be "transformed by the renewing of your mind, that ye may prove what is that good, and acceptable, and perfect, will of God."

The word "transformed" is the same word as is used in the incident where we read that Peter, James and John were together on the mountain top with Jesus when He suddenly was transfigured before them. Transfigured and transformed are translations of the same Greek word. This transfiguration of our Lord and Saviour was seen in that His face shone as the sun and His clothing was white as light. No human being could perform such a transformation by mere human effort. It was in the realm of the divine. The same is true in the case of our spiritual transformation. When a man accepts the Lord Jesus Christ as personal Saviour something happens within that man. He is born again. He is a new creation. Then, when he turns his whole life— including his body—over to Christ, that inner transformation begins to manifest itself in the outward things of the life. But the change is first inward before it is outward.

The Changing of the Mind

In Romans 12:2 we are told that we are transformed by the renewing of our minds. What we think about is basic to what we do. Proverbs 23:7 says, "For as he thinketh in his heart, so is he." Our emotions and actions and reactions all spring from the attitude of our minds. It is essential then, that our minds be renewed.

Because of the new birth, we have the mind of Christ (I Cor. 2:16). His mind has been planted within us, but it must be expressed through our submission to God. God has placed love within us but many Christians do not love. That is why God tells us here to present our bodies to Him—our whole beings to Him —as a living sacrifice, separated entirely to Him. But the work begins in the heart and in the mind, and the mind of Christ has been given us to make this possible.

We read in the eighth chapter of Romans that they that are after the flesh do mind the things of the flesh, but they that are after the Spirit, the things of the Spirit. To be carnally minded is to be minded after this world or this age, and it brings death. Spiritual death, not physical death is thought of here. To be spiritually minded is life and peace. To have our minds under His control results in the fruit of the Spirit being seen in our lives. From this, we see how important it is that our minds be transformed.

Memory Assignment:
Memorize Romans 12:1

EXAMINATION

Complete the following.

1. The phrase, "mercies of God," refers to the _____ _____ in Romans.

2. When we learn what Christ has done for us, we should state as Paul did, "the love of Christ _____ us."

3. The phrase, "By the mercies of God," could also be translated, "_____ _____ the mercies of God."

4. To "present" our bodies means to put our bodies at God's _____.

5. The old nature is part of the old, unregenerate life which seeks to control the body in order to _____ _____.

Circle the correct letter:
6. The body itself is
   a. evil.
   b. neutral.
   c. good.

7. Living in the attitude of being dead to sin and alive to God is
   a. impossible for the Christian.
   b. possible only for a victorious few.
   c. the basis for New Testament Christian living.
8. When we present our bodies to the Lord, we can be assured that God will
   a. remove all sin from them.
   b. accept them as holy.
   c. keep them from sickness.
9. In the Book of Malachi it is recorded that God denounced the Israelites for
   a. not making any offerings to Him.
   b. sacrificing too many animals.
   c. not giving their best in the sacrifices.
10. Instruction for giving to the Lord's work is found in
    a. Acts 16.
    b. Romans 16.
    c. I Corinthians 16.

True or False:

11. _____ Because of all that God has done, it is a reasonable service for the Christian to yield his body to Him.
12. _____ The fact that some places in the world have not been evangelized indicates that God has not called laborers to work there.
13. _____ Worldliness is only seen in the deeds of Christians or the way they dress.
14. _____ The word "transformed" is the same word as "transfigured" in the account of the Lord's transfiguration.
15. _____ A Christian becomes transformed by the renewing of his mind.

☐ I have memorized Romans 12:1.

unit 12

The Illustration of the Body

The third verse of Romans 12 reads: "For I say, through the grace given unto me, to every man that is among you, not to think of himself more highly than he ought to think; . . . God hath dealt to every man the measure of faith." From there, the apostle goes on to show that certain gifts are distributed among God's people, and that the individual capacity for exercising these gifts is according to the measure of faith given by God.

The illustration of the body is then brought clearly into view: "For as we have many members in one body, and all members have not the same office: So we, being many, are one body in Christ, and every one members one of another. Having then gifts differing according to the grace that is given to us, whether prophecy, let us prophesy according to the proportion of faith" (12:4-6). The same truth is set forth in I Corinthians 12:12-20.

Many Members But One Body

Although each organ of the body, or member of the body, has its own particular function, it is nevertheless interdependent upon other parts of the body. For example, the lungs take in air, and from the lungs the blood picks up oxygen and transports it to all parts of the body. In this way the lungs and the heart work in close harmony; the one is of no use without the other. If our lungs ceased to function for just a few minutes, we would die.

In the spiritual sense, we as believers in Christ belong in one body. The Lord Jesus Christ is the Head of the body. He gives it life, and He directs and stimulates, through His Holy Spirit, every member of the body, so that it functions properly.

The Great Essential

Obedience to the Holy Spirit, then, becomes essential for each member of the body to fit perfectly into the body, and to work in harmony with the rest of it. Our life is from Christ, the Head, and that life operates by means of the Holy Spirit in and through the various members of the body.

To grasp this truth fully will mean that there will be less friction, less quarreling and fewer question marks with regard to the way God is using some of His servants. And yet, there are Christians who do not believe that any Christian doing something different than they are doing is in the will of God.

This line of thinking seems to be found in almost every avenue of Christian service. There are some missionaries who cannot imagine that anyone could be in the will of God unless he is a missionary. There are some evangelists who think that anyone in the will of God must be an evangelist.

Prophecy as a Gift

It is essential, then, that we think of the Body of Jesus Christ as composed of those with different gifts. In fact, this is exactly what the Apostle Paul indicates in Romans 12:6, where he says, "Having then gifts differing according to the grace that is given to us, whether prophecy, let us prophesy according to the proportion of faith." Prophecy is only one of many gifts and, of course, is to be used for the purpose intended by God. Foretelling is not its main purpose. It is more particularly the presentation of God's truth to people. Some people have the God-given ability of digging into God's Word and presenting it in such a way that God's people are helped by it. This is a special gift from God, and anyone who has it is to use it to the glory of God.

Gifted for Specific Tasks

From prophecy, the apostle goes on to ministry. "Let us wait on our ministering" (v. 7), he says. There are some who are good evangelists or preachers, and some who are Bible teachers, but they have little ability when it comes to administration. They try to minister the Word according to the gift given them, and at the same time to administer some type of Christian enterprise, but fail in the latter. The reason is that God has given gifts to certain men, and when they seek to do a work outside the realm of these gifts they will not be successful. When God calls a man to do certain work, He gifts that man according to the call given him.

The next gift mentioned is that of teaching. Exposition of the Word is possibly the thought here, and those who have the gift should cultivate it and use it to the utmost.

Following that, we have the word "exhortation" (v. 8). The one who exhorts, or who has the gift of exhortation is to concentrate on that particular gift. This, of course, must be done on the basis of the Word. The truth we find in the Word becomes the foundation for the appeals we make to God's people to follow Him. It must be, however, what the Word says, and not our own thoughts or desires.

Grace of Giving

The subject of giving is next presented, and it is to be done with "simplicity." Not all can be administrators in God's work or expositors of the Word, or pastors, or even exhorters, but God may have given them the gift to make money. This is not for themselves, however, but for His purposes. God gifts some of His servants to earn much money in order that they might distribute it with an eye single to His glory. That is what it means when it says, "He that giveth, let him do it with simplicity." If God has given you the ability to make money, He has done it because He wants you to help meet the expenses of the spiritual ministry one of His other servants is performing.

Ruling and Showing Mercy

The one who rules is to do it with "diligence." The person who has others to direct in their service is to stimulate them with his own enthusiasm for the work. Here again, not all are gifted alike. Some do not have the ability to rule well. But God has gifted all of us so that if we will do faithfully what He expects us to do, the work of God will proceed harmoniously. And the man who does rule is not to lord it over God's people. He is not to be a tyrant, but to inspire the others with the enthusiasm which God has put in his own soul for the work.

One more gift is mentioned here: "He that sheweth mercy, with cheerfulness." There are some who have the ability to bring sympathy to those who are in sorrow. If that is your gift, then bring that sympathy, as Arthur S. Way translates it, "with God's sunlight in your face." Encourage those in sorrow and in trouble. Do not be guilty of pouring your own troubles into their already troubled hearts. Go to them with the sunlight of the Son of God in your face.

Brotherly Love

In verse 9 we come to a very important matter. "Let love be without dissimulation." Let there be no imitation in your Christian love. There should be no hypocrisy about our love. It should be genuine. Such love is the love of God that is shed abroad in our hearts by the Holy Spirit, as we read in Romans 5:5.

Paul goes on to say, "Abhor that which is evil; cleave to that which is good." Let there be a real break with evil. Do not look at something sinful and say, "I wish I could do that, but I'm a Christian, and I guess I can't." Make a genuine break with evil, once and for all.

"Be kindly affectioned one to another with brotherly love; in honour preferring one another" (v. 10). Surely at all times there should be kind affection between Christians as brothers in one family. This, however, is not always true, so Paul says, "In honour preferring one another." There should be a willingness to let the other man have the credit for that which you have been working. In personal honor, put one another to the front. This is often very hard to do, because we are human.

"Not slothful in business; fervent in spirit; serving the Lord" (v. 11). Do not let your zeal slacken, nor let your earnestness diminish. Always be on fire for the thing which God has given you to do.

True Happiness

"Rejoicing in hope; patient in tribulation; continuing instant in prayer" (v. 12). If you want happiness, base it on the hope that you have in Christ Jesus, not on the things you have in your hands. Some people think that they will be happy if they have a nice home or other material possessions. Let our happiness be based upon our hope in Jesus Christ.

Our happiness should be what we have in Jesus, and then it will be everlasting. We may not have all the lovely things we would like to have, but we can have real happiness, because we have Christ. This verse also speaks about prayer. We are to maintain, steadfastly the habit of prayer.

"Distributing to the necessity of the saints; given to hospitality" (v. 13). God has entrusted a few material things to each of us. He wants us to be generous in our giving to other believers and unselfish in sharing our homes with Christians in need.

Notice verse 14: "Bless them which persecute you: bless, and curse not." This is not the human way. God's way to meet adversaries is to bless them. If there is any punishing to be done, let God take care of that. Note verses 19 and 20. An attitude such as this will make us sweeter Christians.

"Rejoice with them that do rejoice and weep with them that weep" (v. 15). Be all things to all men, that by all means you might win some. This can be done without compromise. Evangeline Booth could not win a certain fallen woman to Christ until she put her arm around her and pressed her close to her bosom. Standing at arm's length did not convince the sinner of Evangeline Booth's love, but the arm around her body did.

Verse 16 is very important. "Be of the same mind one toward another. Mind not high things, but condescend to men of low estate. Be not wise in your own conceits." The thought here is that we should live in harmony with each other—be of one heart and one soul. "Mind not high things, but condescend to men of low estate." By this he means that we should be glad to associate with anyone. Do not be "stuck up," but take a real interest in ordinary people. Walk hand in hand with the lowly. Do not be exclusive. Paul says, "Be not wise in your own conceits." In other words, do not be self-opinionated. We should not feel that our opinion and judgment are infallible. We ought not think too highly of ourselves or overestimate our own discernment. Do not be conceited.

"Recompense to no man evil for evil. Provide things honest in the sight of all men" (v. 17). Do not pay back one bad turn with another. Naturally, that is what we would like to do, but God says, "Don't do it."

The second phrase, "Provide things honest in the sight of all men," means "Don't feel that it does not matter what people think." See that your public behavior is above criticism. See that your affairs are handled right in the sight of all men. Have a conscience void of offence toward both God and man.

"If it be possible, as much as lieth in you, live peaceably with all men" (v. 18). The phrase, "As much as lieth in you," means, "So far as it depends upon you." We are to live at peace with all men if possible, but we are not to sacrifice the principles that God has laid down. This puts the responsibility on us.

"Dearly beloved, avenge not yourselves, but rather give place unto wrath: for it is written, Vengeance is mine; I will repay, saith the Lord" (v. 19). We never are to seek revenge for wrongs done to us. We are to leave the field clear for God's wrath. He can take care of it and do a much better job than we can.

"Be not overcome of evil, but overcome evil with good" (v. 21). We should not allow ourselves to be overpowered by evil, but take the offensive ourselves and overpower evil with good. This is a good admonition from the Lord. Too many Christians live defensively instead of being on the offensive.

Memory Assignment:
Memorize Romans 12:5.

EXAMINATION

Circle the correct letter:

1. The Christian's responsibility to other Christians and to Christ is illustrated in Romans 12 by a
   a. temple.
   b. vineyard.
   c. body.
2. In the illustration in Romans 12, all Christians are considered as
   a. one member.
   b. many members.
   c. nonmembers.
3. The gift of prophecy involves "foretelling," but it also includes
   a. presentation of God's truth for the present.
   b. the gift of administration.
   c. the grace of giving.
4. The gift of administration is given to
   a. all Christians.
   b. only ministers.
   c. only certain Christians.
5. The person with the gift of exhortation is to exhort on the basis of
   a. his own thoughts and desires.
   b. what his church teaches.
   c. what the Bible says.

Complete the following.

6. The one who gives with an eye single to God's glory fulfills the scriptural injunction to give with _____.
7. The person who rules is to do it with _____.
8. When encouraging the sorrowing, we should never pour our _____ into their already perplexed hearts.
9. The Christian is to make a genuine _____ with evil, once and for all.

10. True happiness must be based on the _____ we have in Jesus Christ (Rom. 12:12).

True or False:
11. ____ According to Romans 12:13 God wants us to be especially concerned about the needs of other Christians.
12. ____ "Bless them which persecute you," is the human way of responding.
13. ____ Being all things to all men means that sometimes we have to compromise our standards.
14. ____ The Christian should be glad to associate with anyone.
15. ____ The Christian should have a defensive attitude towards others.

☐ I have memorized Romans 12:5.

unit 13

Responsibility to Nation and Neighbor

In chapter 13 of the Book of Romans we have two definite thoughts—our relationship to our government and our relationship to our neighbor. The first seven verses deal with our relationship to our government.

Civil Authorities

"Let every soul be subject unto the higher powers. For there is no power but of God: the powers that be are ordained of God. Whosoever therefore resisteth the power, resisteth the ordinance of God: and they that resist shall receive to themselves damnation" (vv. 1,2).

God says that the higher powers or governments are here by His permission. These civil authorities have been established by Him, directly or indirectly, and so everyone who resists authority sets himself against what God has established.

What should our attitude be toward our government? God says that we should be in subjection to it. There is a difference between the word "subject" and the word "obey." The word "subject" means "submit." Therefore, we are to submit ourselves to them, and if we resist governmental authority, we are resisting the ordinance of God.

Being Subject to Authorities

You may be thinking, "Suppose that those in authority ask something of me that is absolutely against my conscience and against the Scriptures. What shall I do then?" God says that you must be subject to them. What does He mean? Let us consider the example of the apostles. The apostles, in their day, after Christ had gone, were under the authority of certain higher powers. These higher powers decided that the apostles were not to preach in the name of Jesus Christ.

What did the apostles do? They said, "We cannot stop preaching concerning this Man. We must preach Jesus Christ and Him crucified, but we will subject ourselves to you." So they submitted to imprisonment, and they took beatings. Some of them were stoned and some of them were even beheaded. They did not resist when it came to punishment. They accepted it and kept right on preaching the gospel of Jesus Christ as long as they were granted life. The example of the apostles illustrates what is meant by being "subject unto the higher powers."

Let us take a specific instance. Paul was brought before the rulers. He even preached the gospel to them and in such a way that the gospel was heard in all places. But he did not resist them. If they wanted to put him in prison, he let them. He was submissive to them in every respect.

In being subject to civil authorities, there may be certain orders which we feel we cannot obey. Our consciences will not permit us to do so. Suppose that I lived under a Communistic government and was told not only to stop preaching Jesus Christ but also to kill anyone who does preach Christ. What should I do in that case? All I could do would be to simply submit myself to the government and let them cut off my head. If my conscience or the Word of God did not permit me to do certain things which they commanded, then I could still give myself in subjection to their judgment and the punishment that might come as a result.

For the most part, in this passage God is talking about good government that He has especially put here for a purpose. God's Word says, "For rulers are not a terror to good works, but to the evil. Wilt thou then not be afraid of the power? do that which is good, and thou shalt have praise of the same: For he is the minister of God to thee for good" (vv. 3,4). God has permitted the government to be here, and He has a place for civil authority. Civil authority is not a dread to a man who does right, but it is to the man who does wrong. If you do not want to dread the authorities, then practice that which is right. That is the way God calls upon you to act, and you will be commended by the civil authorities if you do so, for they are God's servants to you for good.

Protection of the Law

In my own country I have the freedom to go forth and speak, even though some of the things I say may be contrary to those in authority. I have the right of free speech. That is what God says He has ordained government for, and not only for that, but also to protect us. If some hoodlums should come along, the government is to be there to protect us. Paul appealed for a hearing before the Emperor in Rome on the basis of his Roman citizenship. He was granted protection and safe delivery to Rome, although it turned out that he was killed several years later by a Roman despot.

Civil authorities are God's servants for good, but if we practice doing wrong, we should dread them. "But if thou do that which is evil, be afraid; for he beareth not the sword in vain: for he is the minister of God, a revenger to execute wrath upon him that doeth evil" (v. 4). They wield the sword of God. God permits them to do that, and they are, therefore, the ministers of God. This Scripture supports the idea of capital punishment. We hear much talk against it these days, but Christians should remember that it is suggested here and definitely referred to in Genesis 9:5,6.

"Wherefore ye must needs be subject, not only for wrath, but also for conscience sake" (v. 5). We are to be subject, not only because they have the privilege of exercising wrath, but also for our own conscience's sake.

Taxes

"For this cause pay ye tribute also: for they are God's ministers, attending continually upon this very thing" (v. 6). Most of us do not like to pay taxes and it is possible to be overtaxed, but it does take money to run a government. Jesus paid taxes (Matt. 17:24-27). Why should not we do so?

And then we are told that we should fear and honor those to whom fear and honor are due. These are the things which God emphasizes, and I believe that they are so plain that we need not go into any further detail.

Practical Christianity

Our attitude toward our fellowman and our neighbor is something we need to consider. A good and proper attitude and doing good deeds does not make one a Christian, but if one is a child of God this is a part of the practical side of the Christian life.

"Owe no man any thing, but to love one another: for he that loveth another hath fulfilled the law" (v. 8). This is a very important admonition. God says, "Don't owe anything."

"But," you say, "I am buying a house on time payments. What about that?" If you have a legitimate note or a mortgage on your house you could say that you owe no man anything providing you make your payments as they come due. But if you let your payments become delinquent, then you owe. Paul says, however, that the thing we do owe and should continue to owe men is love, "For he that loveth another has fulfilled the law."

In verse 9 we find a few of the Ten Commandments. "For this, Thou shalt not commit adultery, Thou shalt not kill, Thou shalt not steal, Thou shalt not bear false witness, Thou shalt not covet; and if there be any other commandment, it is briefly comprehended in this saying, namely, Thou shalt love thy neighbour as thyself." Perhaps you feel that you have fulfilled these rules, and, therefore, you are a Christian. Such a conclusion is in error and not in harmony with God's Word.

Verse 10 is important. "Love worketh no ill to his neighbour: therefore love is the fulfilling of the law." If you love your neighbor as you love yourself, you will not do anything to hurt him. You do not plan to harm yourself, because you love yourself too much. Ponder this. If you really love your neighbor as yourself, you will do nothing to harm his soul, his body, or his possessions. In fact, you will think of ways to help him. Love is the perfect satisfaction of the Law.

Time to Awaken

Now we come to something which is particularly important. "And that, knowing the time, that now it is high time to awake out of sleep: for now is our salvation nearer than when we believed" (v. 11). These words were written many hundreds of years ago, but if they had been written today they could not have been more pointed, because they fit right into today's situation.

God says, "The night is far spent, the day is at hand" (v. 12). Now is the time. Our greatest opportunity to get the gospel out is now. We should use every moment, knowing that the present crisis could be the last. Satan's business is to keep Christians from doing God's will. He accomplishes this by rocking them to sleep. Many Christians have become his victims and are fast asleep. They are thus unable to take advantage of the opportunities afforded them. Why is it that we are having to fight war against certain powers and governments? Simply because we did not take these nations the gospel when we had the chance.

There are many open doors today for the gospel. For example, God has ordained gospel broadcasts that we might reach the masses with the Good News. If we do not awake from our sleep and accept the challenge that we have today, we are going to find ourselves in a worse position tomorrow than in 1941-1945.

"The night is far spent, the day is at hand: let us therefore cast off the works of darkness, and let us put on the armour of light" (v. 12). Let us refrain from doing the things that men do in the dark, and let us arm ourselves for the fight of the day. Let us spend our time and money in preaching the gospel.

If we do not treat God right in regard to our finances, He will see that our money is taken away. We are to give Him His rightful share. If we do not, we will lose it in doctor bills, poor crops, or in any of a number of ways. He will see that we are disciplined, so that we will not be able to steal what belongs to Him.

Stewardship

"Let us walk honestly, as in the day; not in rioting and drunkenness, not in chambering and wantonness, not in strife and envying. But put ye on the Lord Jesus Christ, and make not provision for the flesh, to fulfill the lusts thereof." This does not mean that we should not have homes, or that we should not have sufficient clothing, or that we should not have sufficient food. It means that we should not be attached to earthly things. We should not love them more than God or spiritual things.

Such an attitude would be an invitation to the flesh to control our lives. We are living in very serious days. We have a crisis before us. It is time that we should live clean lives, as becoming "daytime," and delight ourselves in the things of God —not in quarrelings and jealousies, which belong to the "night." The Devil has many ways of keeping Christians occupied and busy with themselves, bickering and backbiting. There is so much carnality among Christians that many of them do not take time to do God's work.

It is time that we awake from our sleep. God says that the time is at hand. The night of the age is far spent. The day is dawning just before us when Jesus Christ will come and relieve us from this world of sin. Many thousands are still dying in sin. We have a great Saviour; we have a great opportunity; we have a great privilege; we have a great ministry. Let us be up and working while there is still time.

Memory Assignment:
Memorize Romans 13:1.

EXAMINATION

True or False:

1. _____ The first seven verses of Romans 13 deal with our relationship to our neighbor.

2. _____ All higher powers or governments have been established by God's permission.

3. _____ The word "subject" and the word "obey" are synonymous in their meaning.

4. _____ The apostles kept on preaching and did not subject themselves to the civil government.

5. _____ Paul preached the gospel everywhere he could and at the same time was submissive to the government.

Complete the following.

6. God has appointed rulers to be a terror to _____ works.

7. Paul appealed for a hearing before the emperor in Rome on the basis of his _____ _____.

8. It is only right that a Christian pay _____ to his government.

9. A Christian is not to owe _____.

10. "Love worketh no _____ to his _____."

Circle the correct letter:

11. By loving our neighbor we fulfill the Law. This truth is seen in Romans 13,
    a. verse 7.
    b. verse 10.
    c. verse 14.

12. The greatest opportunity for getting the gospel out
    a. was in the first century.
    b. was during the Reformation.
    c. is the present time.

13. According to Romans 13:12, the Christian is to put on
    a. Christ.
    b. good works.
    c. the armor of light.

14. The Christian is not only to walk as in the day, but he is also to walk
    a. honestly.
    b. proudly.
    c. with anxiety.

15. Romans 13:13 indicates that we should not
    a. plan ahead for earthly needs.
    b. love earthly things more than God.
    c. buy the best quality food and clothing.

☐ I have memorized Romans 13:1.

unit 14

The Law of Love—
Practical Applications

In Romans chapter 14 we have a very practical application of the law of love—the love that is placed in our hearts to reveal itself to others so that they may know that we have something real within us.

Doubtful Things

The law of love makes impossible our indulgence in doubtful things. There are some things which we may believe are not wrong, and they may not be wrong in themselves, but they may be stumblingblocks for others who have weaknesses that we do not have. Too many Christians are unconcerned about others. They are too much concerned about their own rights. We do have our own rights, but we need to remember the message of I Corinthians 13:5: "Love . . . seeketh not her own." True love does not seek its own rights.

This law of love, the attitude that will constrain us in regard to the weaknesses of others, is a Spirit-wrought fruit. This applies to Christians only. If you are a child of God, His love is worked out in you. We read in II Corinthians 5:14: "For the love of Christ constraineth us."

If there is no desire within you to live a separated, godly life, then I feel confident, and I am sure the Scriptures are plain on this matter, that you must not be a child of God. Most certainly you cannot become a child of God by doing the things under discussion here, for these things are the result of being (not the means of becoming) a child of God. There is much confusion as to what constitutes a Christian. In thinking about the new birth we need to consider both the way of salvation and the results that follow. We have discussed how to be born again in earlier units in this course. Now we are discussing the results that follow when we are born again.

Receiving the Weak

"Him that is weak in the faith receive ye, but not to doubtful disputations" (v. 1). Paul means that we should welcome a man whose faith may be weak, but not with the intention of arguing over his scruples. There are people who may not be settled in their minds about some things, but even though they have these doubts, this does not mean that we should not welcome these individuals into our group. If they have not matured in the faith, if they have not been able to see from God's Word that "faith worketh all things," and they still have their scruples, we should, even so, welcome such persons. We should not argue with such people. We should give them the Word of God, and we will find that it will eventually encourage their faith.

"For one believeth that he may eat all things: another, who is weak, eateth herbs" (v. 2). Some are vegetarians, and some are not. Some people say it is wrong to eat meat, while others say that it is not. Paul is discussing this one subject, probably because someone at Rome had written him (at least word had come to him) that there were people who had scruples about this matter of eating meat.

I can understand that. My father was a missionary among the Hopi Indians in Arizona. Once a month these Indians had a feast sponsored by a certain clan. When they came together for the feast they would have a lot of meat, but the meat would be dedicated to idols that they were worshiping. Our parents instructed us that, if we were invited by some of the heathen to go to the feast and eat some of the meat, we were not to do it. They explained to us that it was not wrong to eat such meat as far as we were concerned, but that there were some Christians among the Indians who would stumble over the very fact that we were partaking of things dedicated to idols. So we were taught to leave it alone.

That is what the Scriptures teach us. For the sake of a weaker brother, we should leave some things alone. This was regarding meat, but it may apply to many other things. There are some people to whom certain amusements do not seem wrong, but to others they do. It is the Christian's business to honor the weaker man's faith. If you have more faith, and if you have a clear understanding of the liberty of a Christian under grace, and you feel that you are all right, then do not lord it over the other fellow, but give way to his weakness. It may not always be that he is weak in the faith—it may be that you are. Consider that and be sure of your action before the Lord.

"Let not him that eateth despise him that eateth not; and let not him which eateth not judge him that eateth: for God hath received him" (v. 3). This works both ways. For example, the one who eats meat should not despise the vegetarian, nor should the vegetarian condemn the one who eats meat. Why should they despise each other? God has accepted them both, and not on the basis of whether they eat meat or whether they do not eat meat. What one eats does not make him a child of God. He becomes a child of God because he accepts what God has done for him—the finished work of Calvary.

The Matter of Judging

"Who are thou that judgest another man's servants? to his own master he standeth or falleth. Yea, he shall be holden up: for God is able to make him stand" (v. 4). We criticize the servant of someone else. But we must realize that God understands the situation and He has the true judgment of that person.

Celebrating Days

"One man esteemeth one day above another" (v. 5). Some people argue that Christ was not actually born on December 25. However, we need to remember that what took place is far more important than the day it happened. To commemorate His birth on December 25 is as good as any other day and better than most.

The Christian's Life—Christ

Verses 7 and 8 say, "For none of us liveth to himself, and no man dieth to himself. For whether we live, we live unto the Lord; and whether we die, we die unto the Lord: whether we live therefore, or die, we are the Lord's." Paul does not say here that we ought to live unto the Lord. He says that if we are the children of God, we live unto the Lord. Whether we die or live, it is unto the Lord. We are not to live or die as self-composed units. We are not our own any longer, and every turn of life links us to God. When we die, we come face to face with Him. In life or in death, we are in the hands of God. Christ lived, died, and rose, that He might be the Lord of both the living ones and the dead ones.

In I Corinthians 6:19 we read: "What? know ye not that your body is the temple of the Holy Ghost which is in you, which ye have of God, and ye are not your own?" Since we are saved, we are not our own. The life we now possess is not our own. "For ye are bought with a price: therefore glorify God in your body, and in your spirit, which are God's."

Since He lives within me, and since I am His property, I have but one thing to do in this world, and that is to live or die for Christ. It is not for me to follow my own desires any longer.

We know that Christ would not tolerate some of the things that we are doing today. Christ did not criticize a weaker brother. He helped him along. He lifted him up. He sat down with sinners because the sinners needed healing and help. He associated with sinners, but the Pharisees could not understand that. They would have nothing to do with sinners.

Christ now lives in us. In Galatians 2:20 Paul says, "Nevertheless I live; yet not I, but Christ liveth in me." And in II Corinthians 5:15 we read, "And that he died for all, that they which live should not henceforth live unto themselves, but unto him which died for them, and rose again." We Christians need to see that the life which we now live is actually His life being lived in us!

The Christian's Reckoning

In verse 10 we read, "But why dost thou judge thy brother? or why dost thou set at nought thy brother? for we shall all stand before the judgment seat of Christ." In connection with this, verse 12 says, "So then every one of us shall give account of himself to God." That is very important to remember. Why should we criticize our brother's actions just because he does not have the faith and strength that we have? We shall all be judged one day—not by each other's standards, not even by our own standards—but we shall be judged by the standards of Christ.

Before God alone, we shall give an account for our own actions and not for those of the other man. I do not have to give an account for you, and you do not have to give an account for me. Before God, I will have to give an account for myself. But Paul's discussion here is about our relationship to our fellowman and how we should treat him and live with him.

"Let us not therefore judge one another any more: but judge this rather, that no man put a stumblingblock or an occasion to fall in his brother's way" (v. 13). Stop turning critical eyes on one another. That is a good admonition, but it is hard to follow. The natural way is always to justify oneself and one's own actions in the face of what others are doing. It is natural to criticize the other fellow, because he does not see or do things our way.

Paul's Closing Remarks

Chapters 15 and 16 of Paul's letter to the Christians at Rome make a final plea for Christian service and fellowship.

The first three verses of chapter 15 continue the subject of the Christian's consideration for his weaker brother: "We then that are strong ought to bear the infirmities of the weak, and not to please ourselves. Let every one of us please his neighbour for his good to edification. For even Christ pleased not himself; but, as it is written, The reproaches of them that reproached thee fell on me." Christ is to be our standard in our consideration of others. He suffered that others might have joy and we who know Him as Saviour should be willing to give up things of personal enjoyment in order to help the faith of a weaker brother.

Brotherly unity is stressed in verses 4-13 of chapter 15. Paul prayed that God would grant those at Rome the ability to be "likeminded one toward another according to Christ Jesus" (v. 5). Paul did not want the Roman Christians to begrudgingly give way to the other Christians and so he asked that God would fill them with "all joy and peace" (v. 13). It is possible for a Christian to do right, but at the same time do it with a bad attitude which is a poor testimony.

In verses 14-33 Paul tells those in Rome of his future plans. At the time Paul wrote to them he was on his way to Jerusalem to "minister unto the saints" (v. 25). In particular, Paul's ministry to the Jerusalem saints was to take them an offering which he had gathered for them on his missionary journey. However, Paul planned to go to Spain at a later time and promised to stop at Rome when he did so (v. 24). Paul did not know that he would be taken to Rome as a prisoner, but even this was used to bring glory to God.

In the final chapter of the Book of Romans Paul sends his personal greetings to his friends in Rome. It is evident from the impressive list of names that Paul had enjoyed close Christian fellowship with these friends and that some of them had even hazarded their lives with and for him. The first 16 verses of this chapter give us special insight into the tenderness of Paul's heart toward those with whom he had labored.

Paul cautions the Christians at Rome to avoid those who make divisions among the Lord's people (vv. 17-19). Those who were with Paul sent their greetings also (vv. 21-23). Tertius sent his own greeting since he served as Paul's secretary in writing the letter (v. 22).

Paul ends his letter with a glorious benediction (vv. 25-27). It is characteristic of Paul's life that his closing statement was that God might receive glory, for it was to this that Paul had committed his life.

Memory Assignment:
Memorize Romans 14:4.

EXAMINATION

True or False:
1. ____ Romans 14 is a doctrinal chapter rather than a practical application of doctrine.
2. ____ If we really love others we will be willing to forgo some of our rights.
3. ____ One becomes a Christian by doing the things listed in Romans 14.
4. ____ We should welcome the person into our group whose faith is weak.
5. ____ Paul had probably received word that the eating of meat offered to idols had become an issue at Rome.

Complete the following.

6. It is the Christian's responsibility to honor the weaker man's

   _____ .

7. Regardless of whether he eats meat or not, the person who has received Christ is _____ by God.

8. Regarding the birth of Christ, the fact that it took place is much more important than the _____ it took place.

9. The Christian's body is the _____ of the Holy Spirit.

10. Since the Christian has been bought with a price, his responsibility is to live in such a way to _____ God.

Circle the correct letter:

11. The phrase, "Nevertheless I live; yet not I, but Christ liveth in me" is found in
   a. Romans 14:22.
   b. I Corinthians 10:33.
   c. Galatians 2:20.

12. The Christian is to judge
   a. his Christian brother.
   b. that he not be a stumbling block.
   c. the motives of others.

13. Our standard for consideration of others is
   a. Christ.
   b. fellow believers.
   c. older Christians.

14. When Paul wrote his letter to the Roman Christians, he was on his way to
   a. Ephesus.
   b. Spain.
   c. Jerusalem.

15. The one who served as Paul's secretary for the letter to the Christians at Rome was
   a. Priscilla.
   b. Tertius.
   c. Timothy.

☐ I have memorized Romans 14:4.

ANSWER KEY

After completing each examination, check your answers with these.
Check memory verses in your Bible.

UNIT 1
1. Sanctified, separated.
2. Separate.
3. Obstacles.
4. Fallen, fleshly or old.
5. Forgiveness.
6. b.
7. c or a.
8. a.
9. b.
10. b.
11. False.
12. True.
13. True.
14. True.
15. False.

UNIT 2
1. b.
2. a.
3. a.
4. a.
5. c.
6. False.
7. True.
8. True.
9. False.
10. True.
11. Confess.
12. Forgiveness, confess.
13. Knowing.
14. Faith.
15. Heart or practical experience.

UNIT 3
1. False.
2. True.
3. False.
4. False.
5. False.
6. c.
7. b.
8. b.
9. b.
10. c.
11. Grace.
12. Newness, life.
13. Faith.
14. Spirit, Christ.
15. Fruit or grace.

UNIT 4
1. False.
2. False.
3. True.
4. False.
5. False.
6. Sinners.
7. God or Christ.
8. Condemnation.
9. Conviction, condemnation.
10. Wrong.
11. c.
12. b.
13. a.
14. c.
15. b.

UNIT 5

1. Condemnation.
2. Spirit of life.
3. Principle.
4. Death.
5. Flesh.
6. True.
7. True.
8. False.
9. False.
10. True.
11. a.
12. c.
13. c.
14. a.
15. c.

UNIT 6

1. Die, live.
2. Temple, Holy Spirit.
3. Old, sinful or fleshly; new or divine.
4. Submit.
5. Old nature, Satan, world.
6. c.
7. c.
8. b.
9. c.
10. a.
11. True.
12. True.
13. True.
14. True.
15. True.

UNIT 7

1. b.
2. c.
3. a.
4. b.
5. a.
6. Evil.
7. Together.
8. Present.
9. Image, Son.
10. Satan's.
11. True.
12. True.
13. False.
14. True.
15. False.

UNIT 8

1. False.
2. True.
3. True.
4. False.
5. True.
6. Mosaic.
7. Abraham.
8. Sovereignty.
9. Line, Christ.
10. Unrighteousness.
11. c.
12. b.
13. a.
14. b.
15. b.

UNIT 9
1. True.
2. False.
3. True.
4. False.
5. True.
6. Christ.
7. Hypocrisy.
8. Whosoever, call, Lord, saved.
9. Person.
10. Responsibilities, gospel.
11. c.
12. b.
13. c.
14. b.
15. a.

UNIT 10
1. a.
2. c.
3. c.
4. b.
5. c.
6. Gentiles.
7. Believed.
8. Fulness, Gentiles.
9. Restore.
10. Jealousy.
11. False.
12. False.
13. True.
14. True.
15. True.

UNIT 11
1. Preceding chapters.
2. Constraineth.
3. Because of.
4. Disposal.
5. Practice evil.
6. b.
7. c.
8. b.
9. c.
10. c.
11. True.
12. False.
13. False.
14. True.
15. True.

UNIT 12
1. c.
2. b.
3. a.
4. c.
5. c.
6. Simplicity.
7. Diligence.
8. Troubles.
9. Break.
10. Hope.
11. True.
12. False.
13. False.
14. True.
15. False.

UNIT 13

1. False.
2. True.
3. False.
4. False.
5. True.
6. Evil.
7. Roman citizenship.
8. Taxes.
9. Anything.
10. III, neighbor.
11. b.
12. c.
13. c.
14. a.
15. b.

UNIT 14

1. False.
2. True.
3. False.
4. True.
5. True.
6. Faith.
7. Accepted.
8. Day.
9. Temple.
10. Glorify.
11. c.
12. b.
13. a.
14. c.
15. b.

Now consider these Bible study courses

The Bible and World Missions
The vision and burden of missions must come from a knowledge of God's Word, not just a realization of the world's needs. Your life will take on new meaning when you learn what the Bible has to say about world evangelization.

The Art of Personal Witnessing
This course can help you become an effective witness for Christ. Shows God's provision and power for witnessing, the approach to use, and how to follow up the new Christian.

Foundation Studies in Christian Living
Describes the plan of salvation in detail, with helpful instructions for the new Christian. Shows how to become a mature Christian, overcome temptation, and live victoriously.

Available now at your local Christian bookstore.